THE ESSENTIAL CHEESE BOARD BIBLE

365 Days of Tasty and Delightful Cheese Boards for Every Occasion | Creative Pairings and Recipes to Delight your Family

BY

Sophia Victoria Adler

Table of Contents

Introduction

Welcome to the World of Cheese Boards

You've entered the realm of cheese boards, a culinary art that mixes the tastes and textures of different cheeses with a great variety of complimentary accompaniments. The cheese board is a canvas for foodies of all levels. Your taste buds are the final judges, and the choices are as varied as the cheeses on the market.

The Joy of Cheese Compositions

Have you ever marveled at the beauty and flavor of a well-arranged cheese board? Perhaps you've found yourself entranced by the harmony of colors, shapes, and tastes that a thoughtfully curated cheese platter can offer. The joy of cheese compositions lies not only in the culinary satisfaction they bring but also in the artful presentation and the shared experience they create.

Each cheese board is a tale, a taste adventure, and a conversation starter at any gathering. It's a chance to experiment with cheese varieties and produce a visual beauty that's as inviting as it is tasty.

In this cookbook, we encourage you to delve into this realm of cheese compositions, where we'll lead you through the process of constructing wonderful boards that appeal to a varied variety of tastes, preferences, and situations. We hope you'll join us on this adventure! You'll discover the ideal recipe for a cheese board somewhere within these pages, whether your goal is to wow your dinner guests, inject some fun into mealtimes with your family, or just indulge in a satiating snack all by yourself.

How This Cookbook Can Transform Your Culinary Journey

Cheese compositions should be fun and gratifying like cooking. This cookbook makes cooking simpler, more enjoyable, and more engaging for all skill levels. Here's how:

1. **Inspiration and Exploration:** We'll introduce you to the world of cheese boards, offering inspiration and ideas that will ignite your creativity. You'll discover the vast selection of cheeses available and how to pair them for a balanced and precise taste to suit your preferences.
2. **Practical Guidance:** Creating the perfect cheese board is an art that we'll demystify. We'll provide step-by-step instructions, tips, and tricks to ensure your cheese compositions are not only delicious but also visually appealing.
3. **Accessibility:** We understand the importance of convenience and affordability. Our recipes are designed with the everyday home cook in mind. You won't need to scour specialty stores for rare ingredients; everything is easily attainable at your local supermarket.
4. **Diversity and Flexibility:** We celebrate diversity and accommodate many diets. You'll discover dishes for cheese lovers, vegetarians, vegans, and those eager to impress at your next party.
5. **A Culinary Adventure:** This handbook invites culinary exploration as well as recipe gathering. We urge you to try and customize our recipes. You may customize your cheese boards with clever combos and substitutes.

So, welcome to a world of cheese compositions that will not only tantalize your taste buds but also inspire your culinary passion. Whether you're seeking quick and easy options, budget-friendly solutions, or a little culinary adventure, this cookbook has something for everyone. It's time to unlock the potential of your cheese boards and elevate your culinary journey to new heights. Let's dive in and begin the delightful exploration of cheese compositions.

Chapter 1:
The Art of Cheese Boards

Cheese boards, those delightful canvases of flavors and textures, have taken the culinary world by storm in recent years. No longer confined to upscale restaurants, these platters of cheesy goodness have become a staple of gatherings, family dinners, and cozy nights in. In this chapter, we embark on a journey to explore the enchanting world of cheese boards, understanding why they've become the perfect accompaniment for all occasions and how you can master the art of creating them.

Exploring the Cheese Board Concept

Imagine a picturesque wooden board adorned with an array of cheeses, crackers, fruits, and condiments. The colors, shapes, and aromas blend harmoniously, creating a visual and gustatory masterpiece. This is the essence of a cheese board, a culinary experience that goes beyond the ordinary.

A cheese board is a canvas for creativity, a well chosen selection of cheeses, and a variety of accompaniments to excite the taste senses. This sensual experience delights your taste, sight, and touch. Cheese boards celebrate the vast and varied world of cheeses.

But why has the cheese board idea become so popular recently? Versatility is the solution. Cheese boards are versatile and may be used for many occasions. Cheese boards are perfect for wine and cheese evenings, picnics, and family dinners. It works across cultures and diets, making it ideal for different groups.

Why Cheese Boards Are Perfect for All Occasions

Cheese boards are the chameleons of the culinary world. They can be tailored to suit any event, theme, or mood. Let's explore why they are the go-to choice for various occasions:

1. **Casual Gatherings:** When friends or family drop by for an impromptu visit, a cheese board is a quick and impressive solution. It requires minimal preparation and can be put together in a matter of minutes. With a variety of cheeses, crackers, and a few dips, you're ready to entertain.
2. **Date Nights:** For a romantic evening in, there's nothing quite like sharing a cheese board with your loved one. The combination of flavors and the act of feeding each other can be an intimate experience, perfect for setting the mood.
3. **Party Platters:** Cheese boards make for fantastic party platters. Whether it's a birthday celebration, a game night, or a holiday gathering, a well-constructed cheese board will be the star of the show. Guests can graze at their own pace, and you'll spend less time in the kitchen.
4. **Outdoor Adventures:** Planning a picnic, a hike, or a day at the beach? Cheese boards are portable and can be packed with your favorite cheeses, fruits, and finger foods. They add an element of luxury to your outdoor escapades.
5. **Wine and Cheese Nights:** The classic pairing of wine and cheese is a match made in heaven. A cheese board allows you to explore the intricacies of this partnership, enhancing the flavors of both the wine and cheese.
6. **Family Dinners:** Cheese boards are an excellent way to introduce children to a variety of flavors. You can customize boards to cater to their preferences, and they can have fun building their own combinations.

Your Path to Becoming a Cheese Board Maestro

Becoming a cheese board maestro doesn't require formal culinary training or an extensive cheese knowledge. It's about creativity, experimentation, and a passion for flavors. Here's your path to mastering the art of cheese boards:

Start with the Basics: Begin by familiarizing yourself with the core cheeses and accompaniments. Learn about the different cheese styles, such as soft, hard, and blue-veined, and their flavor profiles. Understand how to choose complementary crackers, fruits, and condiments.

Experiment and Personalize: The beauty of cheese boards lies in their versatility. Experiment with different combinations of cheeses and accompaniments to find your personal style. Don't be afraid to get creative and mix and match.

Presentation Matters: The visual appeal of a cheese board is just as important as its taste. Explore various plating techniques, from arranging cheeses in a circle to creating a cascading effect with fruits and crackers. Use fresh herbs and edible flowers to add a touch of elegance.

Balance and Harmony: Achieving a balanced and harmonious flavor profile is key. Ensure that your cheese board offers a variety of tastes, from creamy and mild to sharp and bold. Pair cheeses with complementary accompaniments that enhance their flavors.

Adapt to Occasions: Tailor your cheese boards to suit different occasions. Whether it's a casual family dinner or an elegant soirée, your ability to create the right board for the right moment is a mark of your mastery.

Embrace Continuous Learning: The world of cheese is vast and ever-evolving. Keep learning about new cheese varieties, emerging condiments, and evolving trends. Your journey as a cheese board maestro is an ongoing adventure.

As we delve deeper into the world of cheese boards in the subsequent chapters, you'll gain the knowledge and confidence to craft captivating boards that will leave your guests in awe. So, don your apron, gather your favorite cheeses, and let's embark on this cheesy voyage together.

Chapter 2:
The Cheese Encyclopedia

Common Cheeses and Their Origins

One of the world's most cherished and adaptable foods, cheese, comes in many varieties and tastes. Knowing the popular cheeses and their origins is crucial before starting your cheese board trip. This chapter covers cheese from All-American staples to French elegance and all in between. We'll also describe each cheese and provide a substitute recommendation for rarer ones.

Cheddar: The All-American Classic

Cheddar, often dubbed the All-American cheese, boasts a rich history dating back to the English countryside. This cheese variety originated in the English village of Cheddar, but it found its way to the United States and evolved into a distinctly American creation.

The creamy, nutty, and slightly tangy taste of cheddar is famous. It ranges from mild to very sharp, letting you customize your cheese boards. Extra sharp cheddar has a robust taste, whereas mild cheddar is buttery.

Cheddar can be a versatile addition to your cheese boards. It pairs wonderfully with apples, pears, and crusty bread, making it an ideal choice for an everyday cheese board.

Brie: A Taste of French Sophistication

If you're aiming for an element of French sophistication on your cheese board, Brie is your go-to option. Named after the French region from which it hails, Brie is a soft, creamy cheese encased in an edible white rind. Its flavor profile is mild, with earthy and buttery undertones.

When ripe, Brie is luxurious and velvety, and it spreads beautifully on crusty baguettes or crackers. For a delightful contrast, pair Brie with fresh fruits like grapes and figs, as well as a drizzle of honey.

Gouda: Dutch Delight

Gouda, the pride of the Netherlands, is a semi-hard cheese that holds a special place on cheese boards worldwide. Its nutty and slightly sweet taste makes it an instant crowd-pleaser.

Gouda is known for its distinctive red or yellow wax coating, which not only seals in freshness but also adds to its visual appeal. Smoked Gouda, a variation of the classic, infuses an irresistible smokiness into your cheese boards.

Gouda pairs wonderfully with dark beers, pumpernickel bread, and tangy pickles. Its versatility makes it an essential addition to any cheese composition.

Blue Cheese: Bold and Tangy

Blue cheese, with its bold and tangy flavor, is a cheese lover's dream. Originating from various regions, such as France, Roquefort; Italy, Gorgonzola; and the United States, Blue cheese gets its distinctive flavor from the blue-green mold running through it.

The characteristic tanginess of Blue cheese complements the creaminess of the cheese, resulting in a complex, delightful taste. It's a cheese that demands attention and pairs exquisitely with a variety of accompaniments.

Blue cheese pairs well with honey, walnuts, and artisanal bread. The contrast of sweet and nutty flavors with the cheese's pungency creates a cheese board experience that's nothing short of spectacular.

Parmesan: The King of Grated Cheeses

Parmesan, the "king of cheeses," is a firm, matured Italian cheese. Savory, salty, and umami define its taste. Parmesan has a granular texture and intense taste from 12 to 36 months of ageing.

This cheese is a must-have for any cheese board, offering a bold and gratifying taste. Grate it over pasta, salads, or even enjoy it as shavings on your cheese board. The depth of flavor Parmesan adds to your compositions is unparalleled.

And Many More

The world of cheese is vast, and while we've covered some common favorites, it's important to explore the countless other varieties. From the Swiss Emmental with its iconic holes to the Spanish Manchego with its distinctively rich and nutty flavor, there are cheeses to suit every palate and occasion.

Characteristics of Each Cheese

Understanding the characteristics of each cheese is vital when composing your cheese boards. Whether it's the texture, flavor profile, or visual appeal, each cheese brings something unique to the table.

Texture: A Tactile Delight

The texture of a cheese is like a fingerprint, defining how it feels and behaves when placed on your cheese board. Understanding the texture of a cheese is essential for crafting an artful composition.

- **Soft Cheeses:** Creamy, delicious cheeses are perfect for crackers and toast. Brie and Camembert are silky and encourage dipping.
- **Semi-Soft Cheeses:** Falling between the extremes of soft and hard, semi-soft cheeses are pliable and versatile. They can be sliced or spread, making them adaptable for various applications. Cheeses like Havarti and Fontina fall into this category, offering a delightful textural middle ground.
- **Semi-Hard Cheeses:** With a firmer texture, semi-hard cheeses can be easily sliced or cubed. Their versatility makes them suitable for serving on cheese boards as well as for cooking. Think of Gouda or Edam, which offer a satisfying balance of texture and flavor.
- **Hard Cheeses:** These cheeses are dense and often crumbly. Hard cheeses are excellent for grating and shaving to create fine, flavorful toppings for dishes. Parmesan and Pecorino Romano are prime examples, celebrated for their granular textures that enhance both the taste and aesthetics of your compositions.

Flavor Profile: A World of Tastes

The world of cheese is a treasure trove of flavors, each as distinct as the cultures and regions from which they hail. When it comes to the flavor profile of cheese, you're embarking on a sensory journey.

- **Mild and Creamy:** Cheeses in this category are gentle on the palate, offering a pleasant and subtle flavor. They often possess a creamy texture that complements their mild taste. Chèvre and Fresh Mozzarella fall into this group, appealing to those who prefer a delicate cheese experience.
- **Sharp and Pungent:** On the other hand, bold, strong cheeses stand out. The blue-green mold gives blue cheeses like Roquefort and Gorgonzola a strong, acidic flavor. This cheese is for individuals who like a lasting taste.
- **Nutty and Sweet:** Many cheeses combine nutty and sweet flavors. This includes

gouda and Swiss Emmental, which are sweet and nutty. These cheeses have a great balance for many tastes.

- **Savory and Umami:** Parmesan, the king of grated cheeses, boasts a savory, salty, and deeply umami flavor. Its aged nature intensifies its taste, resulting in a rich and satisfying experience. Parmesan elevates the complexity of your cheese compositions with its depth and character.

Visual Appeal: A Feast for the Eyes

The visual presentation of your cheese board is just as important as its flavors and textures. The color, rind, and internal features of cheeses contribute to the aesthetics of your compositions, creating an inviting and appetizing tableau.

- **Color:** Imagine your cheese board as a painter's palette, with a diverse range of colors that can evoke various emotions and spark excitement. The spectrum of cheese hues is vast, spanning from the pure, milky white of fresh Mozzarella to the deep, rustic orange of Mimolette. Each cheese brings a unique color to the ensemble. Contrasting these colors creates a mesmerizing and appetizing tableau that beckons guests to explore this vibrant spectrum of flavors. The interplay of colors on your cheese board is akin to an artist's masterpiece, where every shade contributes to the overall visual harmony.
- **Rind:** Just like an artist's canvas, the rind of a cheese is a place of creativity and expression. It's not merely a protective outer layer; it's a storyteller. Cheeses can have a rind that showcases a tapestry of unique molds, a natural or washed rind that adds complexity, or a distinctive coating that hints at the cheese's origin or the aging process. The rind's role in cheese is akin to an art gallery's frame, enhancing the cheese's appearance, character, and flavor. It is an integral part of the cheese's identity and contributes to the overall aesthetic appeal of the board.
- **Internal Features:** A well-composed cheese board is more than just a static display; it's a dynamic, multisensory experience. To achieve this, cheese enthusiasts pay close attention to the internal features of each cheese. Marbling, the presence of eyes (holes), and the incorporation of herbs or spices offer layers of visual intrigue.

The marbling in a blue cheese, for instance, resembles the brushstrokes of an artist, creating patterns that are unique to each wheel. Similarly, cheeses with eyes or added ingredients add depth and dimension to the composition. These internal characteristics are the hidden gems within the cheese, providing visual fascination and influencing the overall tasting experience.

As you design your cheese compositions, consider the interplay of texture, flavor, and visual appeal. A well-balanced cheese board delights not only the palate but also the eyes and touch, creating a multisensory culinary experience. Embrace the diversity of cheeses and use their unique characteristics to craft cheese boards that are not only delicious but also visually captivating.

Substitution Guide for Hard-to-Find Cheeses

While it's exciting to explore the wide world of cheeses, you may encounter difficulties finding specific varieties in your local market. Fear not! Our substitution guide will help you identify alternative cheeses that can stand in for the hard-to-find options, allowing you to craft your cheese compositions with ease and confidence.

As you venture further into the art of cheese boards, you'll find that the possibilities are endless, and a deep appreciation for the rich world of cheese will enhance your culinary journey. Stay tuned as we continue our exploration of the cheese universe in the upcoming chapters.

Chapter 3:
Pairing Perfection

Flavor balance is one of the most enjoyable and creative components of cheese board making. To produce a cheese board that amazes your taste buds and visitors, you must master matching. This chapter covers the complexities of establishing balanced and accurate cheese board taste profiles. You'll learn how to match cheeses and find the best combinations for your preferences.

Creating Balanced and Precise Flavor Profiles

Balancing flavors on a cheese board is akin to creating a culinary masterpiece. It involves an intricate dance of tastes, textures, and aromas that harmonize and contrast, ensuring each bite is a delightful experience. Here are some essential tips to help you craft balanced and precise flavor profiles on your cheese board:

1. Consider the Cheese Types

Start by understanding the flavor profiles of the cheeses on your board. Is there a rich and creamy Brie, a bold and tangy blue cheese, or a nutty Gouda? Each cheese type has its distinct characteristics that should be taken into account.

2. The Rule of Three

A common guideline for cheese board composition is to include cheeses from three different categories: mild, medium, and strong. Mild cheeses provide a gentle introduction, while medium cheeses add complexity, and strong cheeses make a bold statement. This balance ensures a dynamic flavor experience.

3. Texture Matters

Texture is as important as taste. Complement creamy cheeses with crunchy elements like nuts or crisp bread, while crumbly cheeses can be paired with smooth spreads or jams.

4. Sweet and Savory Pairings

Achieving balance often involves pairing sweet and savory items. Sweet fruits like figs, grapes, or honey can counterbalance the saltiness of cheese, while savory olives, charcuterie, or pickles add depth to the board.

5. Consider the Whole Palette

Think of your cheese board as a canvas of colors. A variety of colors and shapes, from the cheese and accompaniments, adds visual appeal and the promise of diverse flavors.

Tips for Pairing Different Cheeses

Combining a variety of cheeses may be like solving a complex puzzle or going on an artistic adventure through a universe of aromas and sensations. It's an investigation that may lead to the discovery of flavor combinations that you had no idea existed, taking your taste senses on a pleasurable journey along the way. We have assembled a treasure trove of ideas and tactics that will improve your culinary experiences and open up new frontiers for your taste in order to assist you in mastering the art of cheese pairings. This will allow you to become a cheese matching master.

1. **Contrast and Complement:** Cheese pairing is all about finding that perfect harmony between contrasting and complementing elements. It's like putting together a complex jigsaw puzzle of flavors and textures. For instance, the creamy richness of Camembert can find its perfect match in the crunch of almonds, while the smoky depth of Gouda can be beautifully complemented by the sweet, juicy slices of apple. Contrasting textures and flavors create a symphony for your senses.

2. **Regional Harmony:** Many regions around the world have rich traditions of cheese and food pairings that have been perfected over generations. Exploring these regional pairings is like taking a culinary journey to far-off lands. You might try Spanish Manchego cheese with a dollop of quince paste, a delightful combination that has stood the test of time. Alternatively, indulge in the authentic taste of Italy with some Parmigiano-Reggiano and a drizzle of balsamic reduction.

3. **Consider the Wine:** The romance between wine and cheese is timeless, like two old friends meeting after years apart. When it comes to wine and cheese pairings, it's essential to know your vino. Whites often make a harmonious companion to creamy cheeses, enhancing their velvety textures. Reds, on the other hand, bring out the richness of aged cheese, creating a marriage of robust flavors. Don't forget the refreshing effervescence of sparkling wines, which can be an unexpected delight for your taste buds.

4. **A Touch of Spice:** Just as a dash of spice can transform a dish, it can also elevate your cheese pairings to new heights. Spices, herbs, and condiments can add layers of complexity to the overall experience. Consider drizzling a few drops of luxurious truffle oil over a mild, creamy cheese, or sprinkle some fiery chili flakes on a sharp cheddar to create a tantalizing sensation in your mouth. Experimentation is the key to discovering your unique cheese pairings.

5. **Trust Your Senses:** The ultimate guide to finding the perfect cheese pairing is your very own senses. Trust your taste buds, as they are your most reliable companions on this gastronomic journey. If a combination feels right to you and ignites your taste buds with delight, then it's a pairing that's worth savoring. Your taste preferences are as unique as your fingerprint, so feel free to explore and let your

senses be your guide.

When it comes to cheese, the options for flavor combinations are only limited by your own creativity. You are now well-prepared to begin on a voyage of culinary discovery with these pointers serving as your guide. The adventure lies in determining what satisfies your taste senses, and you are now well-equipped to do so. There is a cheese combination out there just waiting to be relished, whether you're looking for the ideal contrast or a harmonic balance of flavors in your meal. Therefore, take a step into the realm of cheese pairings, and let your taste buds to enjoy the symphony of tastes that are in store for you. Cheers to a successful cheese business!

Finding the Perfect Pairings for Your Tastes

Pairing perfection on your cheese board is a deeply personal and creative journey that allows you to explore an array of flavors and textures to delight your palate. It's all about finding combinations that resonate with your unique tastes and elevate your cheese board to a culinary masterpiece. Here's a detailed guide on how to discover the perfect pairings that suit your preferences:

1. **Taste and Experiment:** Don't be afraid to embark on a culinary adventure by experimenting with different cheese and accompaniment combinations. The world of cheese and accompaniment pairings is vast, and there are no strict rules. Take your taste buds on a journey and try various combinations to see what excites your palate. Whether you prefer the classic pairings or are inclined towards more adventurous ones, tasting and experimenting are key. Perhaps a sharp cheddar with sweet apple slices or a creamy brie with a drizzle of honey will captivate your senses.

2. **Keep a Cheese Pairing Journal:** Consider maintaining a dedicated cheese pairing journal where you record your favorite combinations. This journal can be your culinary companion, helping you document your successful pairings. Include details about the specific cheeses, accompaniments, and any additional notes about the experience. This way, you can recreate your favorite pairings for future

cheese boards and have a tangible record of your cheese-pairing journey.

3. **Seek Inspiration:** Inspiration for perfect pairings can come from various sources. Explore cookbooks, food blogs, and even dining experiences at restaurants. You might stumble upon unexpected pairings that surprise and delight your taste buds. It's a wonderful way to learn from experts and discover unique combinations that you may not have considered on your own. The culinary world is full of innovative and creative ideas to enhance your cheese board.

4. **Explore Cultural Pairings:** Every culture around the world has its own traditional cheese and accompaniment combinations. Take a global culinary tour by exploring cuisines from different countries and regions. Discover the time-honored pairings that have been cherished for generations. From Spanish Manchego with quince paste to French camembert with fresh baguette, the cultural diversity of pairings is a treasure trove waiting to be explored. Incorporating these traditions into your cheese board adds a rich tapestry of flavors and experiences.

5. **Share the Experience:** The process of making the ideal cheese board may be really enjoyable, but the real magic arrives when you get to share it with your loved ones and close friends. In this part of the article, we'll discuss how showing off your cheese board creations to your friends and family may not only help you improve your cooking abilities but also provide for some really unforgettable moments that will live on in both their memories and their palates.

In conclusion, crafting the perfect pairings on your cheese board is a journey of discovery, creativity, and personal taste. Whether you prefer bold and contrasting flavors or harmonious combinations, the world of cheese pairings offers endless possibilities. Experiment, trust your senses, and remember that there's no one-size-fits-all approach. The art of pairing perfection is all about finding what makes your taste buds sing.

Chapter 4:
Plating Like a Pro

When it comes to creating a remarkable cheese board, the old saying "you eat with your eyes first" holds true. The visual presentation of your cheese board is just as important as the flavors themselves. In this chapter, we'll delve into the art of cheese board plating, exploring creative, harmonious arrangements and avoiding common mistakes to ensure that your cheese composition is a feast for the eyes as much as it is for the palate.

The Art of Visual Presentation

The art of presenting a cheese board goes beyond merely placing cheese and accompaniments on a platter. It's about telling a story, creating an experience, and inviting your guests on a culinary journey. Here are some key aspects to consider when crafting a visually appealing cheese board:

1. The Canvas: Choosing the Right Board

Select a serving platter that complements the theme of your composition. Whether it's a rustic wooden board, an elegant slate slab, or a colorful ceramic plate, the choice of the board can set the tone for your cheese board.

2. Balance and Composition

A visually pleasing cheese board strikes a balance between colors, textures, and heights. Ensure a mix of cheeses and accompaniments that create a harmonious composition. Place the larger items first and build around them, considering the overall shape.

3. Color Palette

Incorporate a variety of colorful elements. Cheeses with different hues, fresh fruits, vibrant sauces, and even edible flowers can add a pop of color to your board. The more colorful, the more inviting!

4. Texture Variety

Provide a wide variety of surface textures. Mix cheesy spreads that are smooth and creamy with almonds that are crunchy, dried fruits that are chewy, and crackers that are crispy. The difference in textures on your board makes it more intriguing to look at.

5. Height and Dimension

Elevate some elements on your board to create depth and dimension. Use ramekins or small bowls to hold dips, jams, or olives, and stack cheeses or salumi to varying heights for an eye-catching effect.

6. Framing and Borders

Consider creating a border or frame with ingredients like thin slices of cucumber, radishes, or fresh herbs. This not only defines the board's edges but also adds a refreshing touch.

7. Negative Space

Don't overcrowd the board. Leave some space between items to let the individual components shine. Empty spaces can be just as important as the items themselves.

Creative and Harmonious Cheese Plating

Now that we've built the groundwork for a cheese board that's visually attractive, let's investigate the art of constructing a composition that will really wow your guests and serve as a showpiece for your party. Not only is a well presented cheese board a treat for the taste buds, but it is also a piece of beauty that captures and holds the attention of the viewer. The following suggestions will turn your cheese board into a culinary masterpiece:

1. **Cheese Placement:** Think of your cheese board as a canvas waiting for your culinary artistry. Start by placing your cheeses strategically. Position them in various areas, ensuring a mix of textures, shapes, and flavors. The interplay of soft, creamy cheeses alongside aged, crumbly ones creates a delightful visual contrast that immediately captures attention.

2. **Accompaniments:** Surround your cheeses with an array of accompaniments, such as fresh and dried fruits, nuts, and spreads. Consider the colors of your accompaniments and their placement to achieve a vibrant and harmonious balance. To prevent any accidental mingling of flavors, use small bowls or ramekins for condiments. This ensures they stay neatly contained and don't overshadow the cheeses.

3. **Symmetry vs. Asymmetry:** Plating a cheese board offers the freedom to express your unique style. You can opt for a symmetrical layout, arranging items in a balanced and ordered pattern that exudes a sense of precision. On the other hand, an asymmetrical approach allows for a more organic, free-flowing design. This style showcases your creativity and highlights the natural beauty of the ingredients.

4. **Garnishes and Herbs:** Elevate your composition with fresh herbs, delicate microgreens, and even edible flowers. These not only introduce a striking pop of color but also infuse the board with a delightful aroma. They serve as the finishing touches that transform your cheese board into a visually stunning masterpiece.

5. **Salumi and Charcuterie:** If your board includes cured meats, treat them as essential components of your composition. Neatly fold or roll the salumi and place them strategically between the cheeses and accompaniments. They can act as dividers or bridges between different flavor profiles, enhancing the overall visual appeal.

6. **Crackers and Bread:** Integrate crackers or slices of bread seamlessly into your composition. Position them alongside the cheeses, ensuring they are easily accessible for your guests. Beyond their role as palate cleansers, crackers and bread also serve as structural elements, creating dynamic patterns that add visual interest to your board.

7. **Focal Point:** To truly make your cheese board stand out, consider introducing a captivating focal point. This could be a wheel of brie, elegantly drizzled with golden honey and adorned with crushed pistachios. The centerpiece not only acts as an anchor for your composition but also draws the viewer's attention, inviting them to explore the board in detail.

Your cheese board is a canvas, and you are the artist. Embrace the opportunity to unleash your creativity, using these plating techniques to transform a selection of delicious ingredients into a captivating masterpiece that will not only please the palate but also delight the senses. Enjoy the process of crafting a cheese board that's not just a feast but a work of art.

Fun and Original Arrangements

Now that you've established the fundamentals of creating a fantastic cheese board, it's time to take your presentation to the next level. Unleash your creativity and add a touch of uniqueness that will make your cheese boards unforgettable:

1. **Theme Boards:** Elevate your cheese board game by introducing thematic creations that center around a specific cuisine or occasion. Think of a Mediterranean mezze board featuring olives, hummus, and feta for a taste of the Mediterranean, or a holiday-themed board that showcases seasonal ingredients like cranberries and pecans. Thematic boards not only provide a delightful array of flavors but also offer a visual feast that can't be ignored.

2. **Personal Touch:** Infuse your cheese board with a personal touch by incorporating homemade elements. Elevate your culinary skills by crafting pickled vegetables, chutneys, or infused oils that reflect your unique flavors. These homemade additions not only add a delightful twist but also create a sense of authenticity and care that your guests will truly appreciate.

3. **Custom Cutting:** Experiment with various cutting techniques to add visual interest to your cheese board. Slice cheeses and fruits into different shapes, such as elegant wedges, cubes, or artistic slices. This attention to detail will not only make your board visually appealing but also showcase your dedication to creating a sensory masterpiece.

4. **Cheese Labels:** Enhance the informative and visual aspects of your cheese board by including labels. These labels can introduce your guests to the diverse selection of cheeses on display, providing not only a visual delight but also an educational experience. Knowing what they're tasting can make the cheese adventure even more enjoyable.

5. **Interactive Boards:** Elevate the fun factor by crafting interactive cheese boards. Add elements like honeycombs and honey dippers, enabling your guests to engage in the cheese selection process. You can also include small cheese knives, allowing your friends and family to slice their preferred amounts of cheese and accompaniments. This interactive approach adds an element of playfulness and customization to the cheese board experience.

6. **Seasonal Elements:** Keep your cheese boards fresh and appealing by incorporating seasonal ingredients. In the summer, consider adding an abundance of fresh berries to your board for a burst of color and flavor. In the fall, roast some root vegetables to bring out earthy, comforting tones. By adapting your cheese

boards to the seasons, you ensure that they remain timely and relevant, offering an ever-changing and exciting dining experience for your guests.

These fun and original arrangements allow you to take your cheese board presentation to new heights. With a little creativity and a personal touch, you can transform your cheese boards into captivating works of culinary art that not only please the palate but also engage the senses and spark delightful conversations. So, let your imagination run wild, and make your next cheese board an unforgettable masterpiece.

Avoiding Common Plating Mistakes

When it comes to assembling an enticing cheese board, there's a balance to strike between artful presentation and practicality. While there's ample room for creativity in cheese board plating, there are a few common pitfalls to avoid, ensuring that your cheese board both looks and tastes exceptional. Here are some key considerations:

1. **Overcrowding:** One of the cardinal sins of cheese board assembly is overcrowding. It's an understandable temptation to want to include every delightful ingredient, but less is often more. Overcrowding your board can make it look chaotic and challenging to appreciate each component. Instead, embrace the beauty of negative space – that open canvas on your board can be as enticing as the items themselves. Leave room for your selections to breathe and make a visual impact.

2. **Inadequate Accompaniments:** A common oversight is underestimating the quantity of accompaniments needed. While it's true that cheese is the star of the show, the supporting cast plays a crucial role. Be sure to provide ample crackers, bread, fruits, and condiments for the quantity of cheese on your board. Running out of accompaniments can disrupt the overall experience, so it's better to have some extras on hand.

3. **Cross-Contamination:** Cheese boards are all about harmony, and that includes the flavors. Be mindful of potential cross-contamination. Some cheeses, like pungent blue cheese, have strong flavors that can dominate milder options. To prevent one

cheese from overpowering the others, keep them at a respectful distance from one another. If you're going for diversity, ensure that your cheeses have room to shine individually.

4. **Temperature Control:** Cheese, like fine wine, deserves to be enjoyed at its best. Pay close attention to temperature. Soft cheeses, such as Brie or Camembert, should be served at room temperature to maximize their creaminess. Harder cheeses, like Cheddar or Gouda, can be served slightly chilled for the best texture. Invest in cheese knives and a quality cheese board that can keep your selections at their ideal temperatures.

5. **Inadequate Labeling:** While not a visual aspect, clear labeling is an important practical consideration. If you have guests with dietary restrictions or preferences, providing labels for cheeses and accompaniments can make their experience more enjoyable. It helps them navigate your delicious spread with confidence, knowing what they can and can't indulge in. Moreover, labels add a professional touch to your presentation.

By mastering the art of visual presentation and keeping these considerations in mind, you'll elevate your cheese board game and leave a lasting impression on your guests. Remember, there are no strict rules when it comes to cheese board creation; creativity is your best tool. So, let your imagination run wild as you craft cheese boards that not only taste incredible but also look like works of art, ready to be admired and devoured. Your cheese boards will become a reflection of your unique style and culinary passion.

Chapter 5:
Pantry Essentials

A well-stocked pantry is your secret weapon when it comes to putting up mouthwatering cheese boards and cheese compositions. If you stock your cheese board armory with the essentials, you'll always be ready to make magnificent boards, whether for an unplanned get-together, a quiet night in, or a special event. This is especially important if you want to wow guests at a party.

This chapter is all about the must-have pantry items that will elevate your cheese board game, tips on procuring, storing, and expertly cutting cheese, and guidance on how to make your cheese boards truly exceptional.

Building Your Cheese Board Arsenal

Your cheese board arsenal consists of the pantry essentials that form the foundation of every great cheese composition. These key components will not only complement the cheeses but also enhance their flavors, creating a visually stunning and palate-pleasing experience. Let's explore each element in detail:

1. **Assorted Crackers and Bread:** A variety of crackers and bread is a must-have for your cheese board. From plain water crackers to artisanal baguettes and seasoned breadsticks, these options add texture and crunch, allowing you to scoop up your favorite cheese combinations effortlessly.

2. **Fresh and Dried Fruits:** Fruits bring a delightful contrast to your cheese board. Grapes, apples, pears, and dried fruits like apricots and figs are excellent choices. Their natural sweetness and varying textures complement the savory and creamy profiles of different cheeses.

3. **Nuts:** Nuts are classic companions for cheese boards. Almonds, walnuts, or pecans provide a satisfying crunch and a rich, nutty flavor that pairs beautifully with various cheeses. They also offer a textural contrast to the creaminess of soft cheeses.

4. **Olives and Pickles:** Olives and pickles introduce a delightful briny note to your composition. Include a selection of green and black olives, along with sweet and tangy pickles. These options provide a savory and zesty balance to the rich, salty flavors of your cheeses.

5. **Honey and Jams:** Sweet condiments like honey and fruit jams are essential for achieving a harmonious balance on your cheese board. These elements counter the saltiness of the cheese, creating a delightful flavor interplay.

6. **Mustards and Spreads:** Mustards in various forms, such as Dijon, whole grain, or honey mustard, are excellent for adding a layer of complexity to your cheese board. Additionally, spreads like chutney or hummus bring unique flavors and textures into the mix.

7. **Cured Meats:** Consider using some mouthwatering cured meats like prosciutto, salami, or chorizo on your cheese board in order to boost the taste profile of the dish and provide a tempting touch of saltiness. This will make the cheese board more appealing overall. Not only do these artisanal meats blend wonderfully with the cheeses you've selected, but they also provide a rich tapestry of flavors and textures, which adds an additional dimension of depth to your culinary ensemble.

8. **Vegetables:** To infuse your cheese board with freshness and vibrant colors,

include a variety of fresh vegetables. Cherry tomatoes, sliced bell peppers, tiny carrots, or other crunchy veggies provide a dimension of crispness and color that's not only visually appealing but also palate-pleasing.

By stocking your cheese board arsenal with these essentials, you'll be well-equipped to create a cheese composition that's not only delicious but also visually stunning. The combination of textures, flavors, and colors will make your cheese board a true work of art, perfect for any occasion. So, get ready to embark on your cheese-venture and start building your masterpiece today.

Must-Have Ingredients Always on Hand

Preparing a delectable cheese board is all about embracing spontaneity, creativity, and the joy of sharing with loved ones. To make sure you're always ready for impromptu cheese board adventures, it's crucial to keep a well-stocked pantry and refrigerator with essential ingredients that can elevate your cheese compositions. These staples will ensure that you can craft a beautiful cheese board at a moment's notice. Let's delve into the must-have items that should always be within arm's reach:

1. **Cheese:** Naturally, cheese is the highlight of any cheese board. Keep a variety of cheeses in your fridge to cover tastes, textures, and flavors. Cheddar, brie, and gouda are crowd-pleasers and great cheese board foundations. Also, retain some specialty cheeses, local favorites, or uncommon findings that suit your tastes. A balanced assortment includes soft, semi-soft, and hard cheeses.
2. **Olive Oil and Balsamic Vinegar:** Few things beat high-quality olive oil and balsamic vinegar for complementing cheese and bread tastes. A high-quality olive oil and aged balsamic vinegar may enhance even the most basic things on your board. Drizzle these liquid golds over cheeses and serve with fresh baguette slices to create a culinary beauty.
3. **Fresh Herbs:** Fresh herbs are like aromatic jewels in the world of cheese boards. Keeping a small herb garden or potted herbs on your kitchen windowsill ensures you always have a fragrant and visually appealing garnish for your compositions.

Herbs like rosemary, thyme, basil, and mint can be used to add a burst of color, fragrance, and flavor to your boards. A sprig of fresh rosemary might complement a sharp cheddar, while basil leaves can beautifully accentuate the creaminess of a brie.

4. **Quality Salt and Pepper:** Salt and pepper are the unsung heroes of cheese boards. Whether you're seasoning your cheeses or adding a finishing touch to some olives, a good sea salt and freshly ground black pepper are indispensable. Opt for a high-quality sea salt, such as fleur de sel or Maldon, to add a delicate crunch and a burst of salinity to your compositions. Freshly ground black pepper, with its aromatic punch, can balance the richness of cheeses and enhance their flavors.

5. **Cheese Knives and Cheese Tools:** Serving your cheeses with precision and flair requires the right tools. Invest in a set of dedicated cheese knives, each designed for specific types of cheese, from soft to hard. A cheese wire is excellent for slicing, and cheese markers help your guests identify different cheeses with ease. With these tools, you can create an elegant and organized presentation that showcases your attention to detail.

6. **Cheese Paper or Parchment Paper:** Proper storage is crucial for preserving the freshness and flavors of your cheeses. To prevent cheese from drying out or absorbing unwanted odors in the fridge, keep cheese paper or parchment paper on hand. These protective layers allow your cheeses to breathe while maintaining their optimal texture and taste. When storing leftover cheese after a delightful cheese board evening, wrap it in cheese paper or parchment paper before placing it in an airtight container or resealable bag.

With these must-have ingredients and essentials in your culinary arsenal, you're well-prepared to embark on your cheese board adventures, delighting in the art of spontaneity and creativity. Whether it's a casual weeknight gathering or a special celebration, your well-stocked pantry and refrigerator will ensure you're ready to craft cheese boards that captivate and delight your guests. So, savor the joy of creating, sharing, and relishing in the world of cheese board artistry. Happy cheesemongering!

Buying, Storing, and Cutting Cheese Like a Pro

Buying Cheese

When embarking on the delightful journey of cheese board creation, one of the initial and most crucial steps is the careful selection of the star of the show - cheese. Venturing into the cheese aisle or visiting your local cheesemonger's shop can be a fascinating and sensory experience. Here are some tips to make the most of your cheese-buying adventure:

- **Buy Local:** When you're confronted with a seemingly endless array of choices, it's easy to feel as if you're standing in front of a wall of cheese. Consider beginning with local cheeses, however, if you want to add distinctive tastes to your cheese board and show your support for local artists at the same time. These cheeses often possess particular geographical qualities that are unable to be recreated in any other location. You will not only be doing something unique for your taste senses, but you will also be supporting local cheese makers and helping to maintain the art of traditional cheese manufacturing in your community by doing so.
- **Ask for Samples:** Don't be bashful about cheese selection. Cheesemongers and shop owners know cheese selection is personal and difficult. Most are happy to give you samples to try before you decide. Sampling lets you taste, smell, and feel each cheese. It helps you choose cheeses that match your palette and cheese board theme. Take this chance to sample and learn about the cheeses.
- **Variety is Key:** Remember that cheese variety is the spice of life to build a visually beautiful and diversified cheese board. Choose cheeses with distinct textures and flavours. Include a variety of soft, hard, and semi-soft cheeses in mild, creamy, sharp, and pungent flavors. This variety will satisfy any cheese board visitor.

When selecting cheeses, think about pairing creamy brie with a tangy blue cheese, or a sharp cheddar with a mellow Gouda. Each cheese should bring a distinct personality to your board, contributing to a harmonious and flavorful ensemble. This variety will not only satisfy the palates of your guests but also provide a visually captivating experience, as different colors, shapes, and sizes come together to create a work of culinary art.

In summary, shopping for cheese is an art in itself. The choices you make in the cheese aisle will lay the foundation for a cheese board that tells a unique, flavorful story. Embrace the local offerings, take advantage of sampling opportunities, and remember that variety is the key to crafting an exceptional cheese board. As you curate your selection, you're setting the stage for a memorable culinary journey that all cheese enthusiasts, from the novice to the connoisseur, can enjoy.

Storing Cheese

Proper cheese storage is a crucial aspect of ensuring your cheeses maintain their quality and flavor. Here are some essential guidelines to help you store your cheese effectively:

- **Use Cheese Paper:** The appropriate wrapping is essential if you want to keep the exquisite flavor of your cheeses for as long as possible. Cheese paper, which has been specifically developed for this use, is the superior option. If you don't have cheese paper on hand, you may substitute parchment paper for it and get the same level of success. Protect the individual tastes and fragrances of each variety of cheese by wrapping them in different containers before storing them.
- **Label the Cheeses:** It's easy to lose track of which cheese is which, especially if you're storing multiple varieties. To prevent any confusion, be sure to label the cheese paper with the type of cheese inside. This simple step can save you from unwelcome surprises when you're ready to savor your cheese.
- **Keep It Cool:** Cool temperatures are good for cheese, so keep it in the fridge. The vegetable drawer has somewhat greater humidity than the rest of the fridge, so store cheese there. Most cheeses thrive around 35–45°F (2–7°C). Soft and fresh cheeses may tolerate higher temperatures. Each cheese's storage instructions must be checked.
- **Avoid Airtight Containers:** While it may be tempting to seal your cheese in airtight containers, this can lead to moisture buildup and an unpleasant texture. Cheese needs to breathe, so it's best to use cheese paper or parchment paper

instead of sealing it in plastic or airtight containers. This allows for proper airflow while maintaining the right humidity levels.

- **Regularly Check and Replace Wrappings:** Cheese paper and parchment paper can become damp or oily over time. To keep your cheeses in top condition, periodically check the wrappings and replace them if they appear soiled. This practice ensures that your cheese remains free of unwanted moisture and maintains its flavor.

- **Store Strong-Smelling Cheeses Separately:** Some cheeses, like blue cheeses, have strong and distinct odors that can affect milder varieties if stored together. It's a good idea to keep these potent cheeses in a separate section of your refrigerator or even in an airtight container to prevent their aromas from permeating other cheeses.

- **Allow for Temperature Adjustment:** Before serving your cheese board at a party, take the cheeses from the fridge 30 minutes to an hour. Allowing them to warm may improve their tastes and smells. However, avoid leaving them out too long, particularly in warm weather.

- **Follow Specific Cheese Recommendations:** While these general guidelines apply to many cheeses, remember that some varieties have unique storage requirements. For instance, fresh cheeses like mozzarella or ricotta may benefit from storage in a more humid environment. Always check the specific recommendations for the cheese you have and adjust your storage accordingly.

By following these simple guidelines, you can ensure that your cheese remains in excellent condition and ready to be a star on your cheese board. Proper storage helps maintain the integrity of your cheeses and guarantees a delightful cheese-tasting experience every time.

Cutting Cheese

A tasty cheese board depends on the details, and cheese cutting is frequently disregarded. Believe it or not, how you slice, wedge, or cube your cheese might affect your cheese experience. Key factors for flawless cheese-cutting:

- Cheese Temperatures

Food like cheese may be eaten at various temperatures. The best cheese serving temperature depends on the kind. Brie and camembert are finest at room temperature. This highlights their creamy texture and nuanced tastes. Hard cheeses like aged cheddar or Parmigiano-Reggiano should be served slightly cold. The lower temperature keeps them firm and enhances their sharp, nutty flavors.

Serving cheeses at the appropriate temperature improves their texture and flavor, making visitors happier. Remove cheeses from the fridge before serving to attain their proper temperature.

- Knife Selection

Not all cheeses are created equal, and neither are the knives you should use to cut them. Each type of cheese demands a specific tool for the job:

Cheese Wire: Soft and creamy cheeses like brie, camembert, or fresh goat cheese are best tackled with a cheese wire. This fine wire tool allows for a clean and smooth cut, preserving the delicate texture of these cheeses without sticking or squishing.

Cheese Plane or Slicer: Semi-hard cheeses like Gouda, Emmental, or Edam are most effectively cut using a cheese plane or slicer. These knives feature a flat blade with an adjustable thickness dial, perfect for creating uniform, thin slices of cheese. This method is not only visually appealing but also enhances the cheese's taste by allowing it to melt effortlessly on the palate.

Sharp Knife: When dealing with hard cheeses such as aged cheddar, Manchego, or pecorino, a sharp knife is your best friend. The robust blade can cut through the firm texture of these cheeses without crumbling or splintering, resulting in clean, satisfying chunks or shards.

By choosing the right knife for the cheese, you ensure that each slice or wedge is as aesthetically pleasing as it is delicious.

- **Slice or Wedge:** Consider the cheese's shape and texture when deciding to slice, wedge, or cube.

By having these essential items on hand and mastering the art of buying, storing, and cutting cheese, you'll be well-prepared to create remarkable cheese boards that will impress your guests and satisfy your culinary cravings. With your pantry stocked and cheese skills honed, the next step is to delve into the art of pairing cheeses and other ingredients, which we'll explore in the following chapters.

Chapter 6:
Cheese Meat Beverage

Pairing Cheeses with Beverages

When it comes to putting up the ideal cheese board, one aspect that must never be neglected is mastering the skill of combining different types of cheese with the appropriate drinks. You may take your cheese board experience to the next level by pairing it with beverages, which will result in the creation of a symphony of tastes that will excite the taste receptors. In the next section, we will delve into the realm of beverage pairings and discuss the ways in which these combinations might improve your cheese creations.

Wines: Uncorking the Perfect Match

Wine and cheese have a longstanding romance that dates back centuries. The complexity of wine, with its diverse range of flavors, makes it an ideal partner for cheese. Here, we'll delve into the world of wine pairings and discover how to uncork the perfect match for your cheese compositions.

1. **Red Wines and Cheese:** Cabernet Sauvignon, Merlot, and Pinot Noir match well with old cheeses like Cheddar and Gouda because to their robustness and tannins. Red wine tannins offset cheese's richness.

2. **White Wines and Cheese:** Chardonnay and Sauvignon Blanc go well with Brie and Camembert because to their lighter, sharper flavors. The cheese's creamy texture is refreshed by white wine's acidity.

3. **Sparkling Wines and Cheese:** Sparkling wines, such as Prosecco and Champagne, are a fantastic match for a range of cheeses because of their lively nature. You may taste a wide variety of tastes, from the mildness of fresh cheeses to the intensity of blue cheeses, since the bubbles clear your palette.

4. **Fortified Wines and Cheese:** Fortified wines like Port, Sherry, and Madeira have a sweet and intense character that pairs beautifully with strong, pungent cheeses like Stilton or Roquefort. The sweetness of these wines balances the saltiness and intensity of the cheese.

5. **Regional Pairings:** Explore wine and cheese pairings from different regions around the world. For instance, try Spanish Manchego with a glass of Rioja or pair creamy goat cheese with a crisp Sancerre from the Loire Valley.

Beers: Craft Beer and Cheese Harmony

While wine and cheese pairings are widely celebrated, the world of craft beer offers an exciting alternative. Craft beers come in a diverse range of styles, each with its own unique flavor profile. Here, we'll uncover the secrets of creating harmony between craft beer and cheese on your cutting board.

1. **Lager and Cheese:** The crisp and clean taste of lagers complements lighter cheeses such as Swiss and Mozzarella. The subtle maltiness of lagers adds a pleasant dimension to the cheese's flavors.

2. **IPA (India Pale Ale) and Cheese:** The hoppy and aromatic nature of IPAs pairs wonderfully with bold and flavorful cheeses like sharp Cheddar or aged Gouda. The hops in the beer create a contrast that enhances the cheese's complexity.

3. **Stout and Cheese:** The rich and roasted notes of stouts make them an excellent match for robust and creamy cheeses like Brie or Camembert. The coffee and chocolate undertones in stouts create a delightful pairing experience.

4. **Belgian Ales and Cheese:** Belgian ales, known for their fruity and spicy

characteristics, offer a fantastic partnership with a variety of cheeses. Pair them with semi-soft cheeses like Fontina or Gruyère for a flavorful adventure.

5. **Craft Beer Exploration:** Experiment with local and international craft beers to discover unique and exciting pairings. Craft breweries often produce seasonal or limited-edition brews, making each tasting experience a delightful adventure.

Cocktails: Mixology Meets Cheese

While wine and beer are classic choices for pairing with cheese, mixology enthusiasts can take their cheese board experience to a whole new level by exploring cocktail pairings. Crafted with precision, cocktails can provide a well-balanced counterpoint to the richness of cheese. Let's dive into the world of mixology-meets-cheese.

1. **Classic Martini and Cheese:** The crisp and clean profile of a classic martini, made with gin or vodka and a hint of vermouth, complements delicate and fresh cheeses like Chevre or Ricotta. The martini's botanical notes add an herbal touch to the cheese.

2. **Old Fashioned and Cheese:** The Old Fashioned, a timeless cocktail made with bourbon or rye, sugar, and bitters, pairs harmoniously with aged cheeses such as Parmesan or Gouda. The cocktail's smoky and caramel undertones enhance the cheese's depth.

3. **Margarita and Cheese:** The zesty and citrusy notes of a Margarita, made with tequila, lime juice, and orange liqueur, provide a lively contrast to mild and creamy cheeses like Havarti or Monterey Jack.

4. **Crafting Cheese-Infused Cocktails:** Get creative by infusing cheese flavors into cocktails. Try a Brie and Pear Martini or a Blue Cheese Manhattan for a unique taste sensation.

Enhancing Your Cheese Board Experience

Pairing cheeses with beverages is a journey of discovery, and there are endless possibilities to explore. To enhance your cheese board experience, consider hosting tastings with friends and family, trying different combinations, and savoring the delightful surprises that emerge. Cheers to the wonderful world of cheese and beverage pairings!

Chapter 7:
Cheese Glossary

Explore the World of Cheese Styles and Tastes

When you embark on your cheese board journey, understanding the diverse world of cheese is essential. This chapter serves as your passport to this delectable world, introducing you to various cheese styles, tastes, and textures. From fresh and creamy to crumbly and aged, there's a cheese for every palate and occasion.

Fresh, Soft, Hard, Blue-Veined, and Vegan Varieties

Fresh Cheeses

Mozzarella: A classic Italian cheese known for its soft, milky texture. Mozzarella is a versatile cheese, often used in Caprese salads and as a pizza topping.

Ricotta: A fresh, creamy cheese that hails from Italy. Ricotta is beloved for its mild, slightly sweet flavor, making it a favorite in both savory and sweet dishes.

Goat Cheese (Chèvre): This cheese tastes acidic and earthy. Its creamy or crumbly texture makes it great for salads and spreads.

Soft Cheeses

Brie: A creamy, French cheese with a mild, buttery taste. Brie is known for its edible, white rind and pairs wonderfully with fruits and bread.

Camembert: Another French favorite, Camembert is rich and earthy, often compared to Brie. It boasts a velvety texture and a slightly stronger flavor.

Blue Cheese: Blue cheese varieties like Roquefort and Gorgonzola are characterized by their blue veins. They offer bold, salty, and savory profiles that can be an acquired taste.

Hard Cheeses

Cheddar: A beloved American classic, cheddar comes in a range of flavors, from mild to sharp. Its firm texture and versatility make it perfect for slicing or grating.

Parmesan: This Italian cheese is famous for its nutty and savory taste. Parmesan is often grated over pasta dishes and salads, adding depth of flavor.

Gouda: A Dutch treasure, Gouda comes in various ages, from young and mild to aged and robust. It's known for its buttery texture and sweet, caramel-like undertones.

Blue-Veined Cheeses

Stilton: A revered English blue cheese with a rich and crumbly texture. It offers a complex, sharp, and earthy flavor.

Roquefort: A French blue cheese with a strong, tangy taste. It's creamy, crumbly, and aged in limestone caves, which gives it a unique character.

Gorgonzola: An Italian blue cheese that ranges from mild to intense in flavor. It's creamy, tangy, and often used in dressings or spreads.

Vegan Varieties

Vegan Cream Cheese: Plant-based cream cheese alternatives provide the creamy texture and tangy taste of traditional cream cheese, without dairy.

Vegan Cheddar: For those preferring a strong, savory taste and cheese-like texture, vegan cheddar cheese is an option.

Nut-Based Cheeses: Cashews, almonds, and other nuts are used to make these cheeses. They range from soft and spreadable to stiff and sliceable.

Chapter 8:
Beyond Cheese

Pairing Cheeses with Other Ingredients

Cheese dominates the ultimate cheese platter. The complimentary items make a cheese board memorable. We'll explore matching cheeses with a variety of elements to enrich your cheese board in this chapter.

Sauces: A Saucy Adventure

Trying new sauces to match cheese is one of the most fun parts of making a cheese board. Sweet, savory, or acidic sauces are available for every cheese. Try these naughty activities:

1. **Honey and Cheese:** The classic pairing of honey and cheese is a match made in culinary heaven. The sweetness of honey beautifully contrasts the saltiness of many cheeses. Drizzle honey over your favorite cheese or serve it in a small bowl for dipping.

2. **Fig Jam:** Fig jam adds a delightful sweet and slightly earthy flavor to your cheese board. It pairs exceptionally well with soft cheeses like Brie or Camembert.

3. **Spicy Mustard:** Spicy mustard is your go-to condiment for heat. It complements sharp cheeses like Cheddar and Gouda.

4. **Balsamic Reduction:** A balsamic reduction drizzled over cheese can add a rich, sweet, and tangy element. It pairs nicely with a variety of cheeses, especially those with a milder flavor.

5. **Pesto:** Pesto, with its vibrant green color and bold flavor, can elevate any cheese board. It's a fantastic match for fresh and soft cheeses.

Spreads: Spreading Flavor Joy

Spreads are versatile and can be used in various ways to enhance the cheese board experience. They offer a delightful contrast in textures and flavors. Here are some delightful spreads to consider:

1. **Olive Tapenade:** A savory spread made from olives, capers, and olive oil, olive tapenade adds a burst of briny goodness to your cheese board. Pair it with feta or goat cheese for a Mediterranean twist.

2. **Whipped Ricotta:** Whipped ricotta is light, creamy, and a perfect companion for both sweet and savory cheese boards. Its mild flavor makes it a versatile choice.

3. **Artichoke Dip:** Creamy and rich, artichoke dip pairs wonderfully with harder cheeses. Its mild tanginess complements the cheese's saltiness.

4. **Onion Jam:** A sweet and savory onion jam can add depth to your cheese board. Pair it with blue cheese for a flavor explosion.

5. **Garlic Hummus:** Hummus is a crowd-pleaser that pairs well with a variety of cheeses. Its creamy texture and subtle garlic flavor make it an excellent choice.

Jams: Sweet and Savory Juxtaposition

The world of jams offers a diverse range of flavors that can harmonize beautifully with cheese. Jams provide a sweet and sometimes tangy contrast to the cheese's richness. Consider these sweet and savory jams:

1. **Apricot Jam**: Apricot jam's sweet and slightly tangy notes make it a versatile choice. It complements a wide range of cheeses, from soft Brie to sharp Cheddar.
2. **Cherry Compote:** Cherry compote is a delightful mix of sweet and tart. It pairs particularly well with blue cheese, creating a balanced and flavorful combination.
3. **Quince Paste:** A dense, sweet paste made from quince fruit, quince paste is a classic choice for pairing with Manchego or other hard, nutty cheeses.
4. **Bacon Jam:** Yes, you read that right – bacon jam. This sweet and savory concoction adds a smoky, meaty element to your cheese board. It's an ideal match for aged cheeses.

Breads: Carbs and Cheese Unite

Breads are an essential component of any cheese board, providing a vehicle for enjoying the cheese and its accompaniments. Here are some bread options to consider:

1. **Baguette Slices**: Baguette slices are a classic choice. They offer a crisp crust and a soft interior, making them an excellent vessel for spreading cheese or dips.
2. **Crackers:** There's a wide variety of crackers available, from simple water crackers to multigrain or rosemary-infused options. Choose crackers that complement your cheese selection.
3. **Crostini:** These toasted bread slices are perfect for adding a crunchy texture to your cheese board. They're particularly well-suited for soft cheeses.
4. **Fruit and Nut Bread:** Fruit and nut bread, such as walnut or raisin bread, adds a sweet, nutty dimension to your cheese board. It pairs wonderfully with softer cheeses.
5. **Grilled Sourdough**: Warm, grilled sourdough offers a delightful contrast to the cold cheeses on your board. Its slightly tangy flavor pairs well with a variety of cheeses.

Dried Fruits: Nature's Sweetness

Dried fruits are a fantastic addition to a cheese board, offering natural sweetness and a chewy texture. Consider these options:

1. **Dried Apricots:** Apricots add a sunny, sweet note to your cheese board. They're particularly compatible with milder cheeses.
2. **Figs:** Figs are a classic choice for cheese boards. Their natural sweetness and chewy texture make them an excellent pair for many cheese varieties.
3. **Dates:** Dates are sweet and slightly earthy, making them a great match for salty and sharp cheeses.
4. **Cranberries:** Dried cranberries bring a touch of tartness to your board, balancing the richness of the cheese.
5. **Raisins:** Raisins are a timeless choice, offering a familiar and pleasing sweetness that complements a wide range of cheeses.

Cured Meats: Charcuterie Companions

Cured meats, or charcuterie, are a savory and indulgent addition to any cheese board. They provide a satisfying contrast to the cheese's textures and flavors. Here are some charcuterie options:

1. **Prosciutto:** Prosciutto's delicate, salty, and somewhat sweet taste complements mozzarella and goat cheese.
2. **Salami:** A variety of salamis are available, each offering a different level of spiciness and richness. They're great companions for hard and aged cheeses.
3. **Chorizo:** Chorizo's smoky and spicy character can add a delightful kick to your cheese board. It pairs wonderfully with manchego or other Spanish cheeses.
4. **Coppa:** Coppa is a rich and marbled cured meat with a peppery kick. It's a fantastic choice for accompanying robust, aged cheeses.
5. **Soppressata:** Soppressata, an Italian dry-cured salami, offers a satisfying, spicy note that pairs well with a range of cheeses.

Elevating Your Cheese Board with Complementary Elements

When creating your cheese board, don't shy away from experimenting with these delightful sauces, spreads, jams, breads, dried fruits, and cured meats. The possibilities are endless, and by exploring the world of complementary elements, you'll craft cheese boards that are not only visually appealing but also a feast for the palate.

A balanced cheese board is essential. Flavors, textures, and colors should complement each other. Your visitors will remember your cheese platter if you strike this balance. Complementary parts are great for mixing and matching to create a cheese board that suits your taste or occasion. These pieces will enhance your cheese board for a romantic date, a casual get-together, or a joyful celebration.

So, don your culinary creativity hat and embark on the journey of cheese board creation. Experiment with different combinations, explore new sauces and spreads, and savor the delightful juxtaposition of sweet and savory. Your cheese board will become a work of art that not only tantalizes the taste buds but also leaves a lasting impression on your guests.

In the next chapter, we'll explore the world of 30 cutting board recipes and compositions, each accompanied by a list of ingredients and their accompaniments. Get ready to take your cheese board mastery to the next level with innovative and easy-to-follow recipes that cater to a variety of tastes and occasions.

Expand Your Cheese Knowledge

As you delve into the realm of cheese boards and compositions, exploring various cheese styles and tastes will open up a world of culinary possibilities. Each cheese brings its unique character to the table, and experimenting with different combinations will elevate your cheese board creations.

Remember that this vocabulary is only the beginning. Cheese is large and varied, with regional and artisanal types to explore. A cheese will satisfy your taste buds and inspire your cheese board, whether you like creamy, mild cheeses or robust blue-veined classics. We'll teach you how to combine these cheeses with complimentary components, create magnificent cheese compositions, and improve your cheese knowledge in the next chapters. Your path to cheese board mastery is beginning, and it's fantastic. Let's keep discovering, trying, and enjoying cheese.

Chapter 9:
Cheese Compositions

Quick and Easy Recipes for Cheese Compositions

All American Cheese Board

Servings: 4-6 people | Preparation: 15 minutes

Ingredients:

- 150g (5 oz) American cheddar cheese
- 150g (5 oz) Monterey Jack cheese
- Mini hot dogs or sausages
- Mustard and ketchup
- Pretzel bites
- Pickles
- Sliced apples
- Fresh parsley sprigs

Directions:

1. Arrange American cheddar and Monterey Jack cheeses on your serving platter.
2. Serve mini hot dogs or sausages with mustard and ketchup in small dishes.
3. Add pretzel bites, pickles, and sliced apples to the board.
4. Garnish with fresh parsley sprigs.

Asian Fusion Cheese Board

Servings: 4-6 people | Preparation: 20 minutes

Ingredients:

- 150g (5 oz) Wasabi cheddar cheese
- 150g (5 oz) Nori-wrapped sesame cheese
- Edamame pods
- Pickled ginger
- Soy sauce
- Rice crackers
- Fresh cilantro leaves

Directions:

1. Place wasabi cheddar cheese and nori-wrapped sesame cheese on your platter.
2. Arrange edamame pods and pickled ginger around the cheeses.
3. Offer small dishes of soy sauce for dipping. Serve with rice crackers.
4. Garnish with fresh cilantro leaves.

Carnival Cotton Candy Cheese Board

Servings: 4-6 people | Preparation: 20 minutes

Ingredients:

- 150g (5 oz) Chevre (goat cheese)
- 150g (5 oz) Roquefort cheese
- Lavender-infused honey
- Lavender and thyme crackers
- Dried lavender buds (for visual appeal)
- Fresh lavender sprigs for garnish

Directions:

1. Place Cotton candy-infused cheese, bubblegum and mallow cheese on platter.
2. Serve mini carnival cotton candy cones and colorful gummy candies in a fun dish.
3. Add candy floss clouds, marshmallows, candy sprinkles for extra sweet touch.

Classic Cheese Board

Servings: 4-6 people | Preparation: 15 minutes

Ingredients:

- 150g (5 oz) Brie cheese
- 150g (5 oz) Cheddar cheese
- 150g (5 oz) Gouda cheese
- 100g (3.5 oz) Prosciutto or other cured meat
- 1/2 cup (60g) mixed nuts (almonds, cashews)
- 1/4 cup (85g) honey
- 1 bunch of grapes
- 1 baguette, sliced
- Fresh rosemary sprigs for garnish

Directions:

1. Arrange the cheeses on a large cheese board or platter.
2. Fold the slices of prosciutto into attractive shapes and place them around the cheese. Scatter mixed nuts across the board, focusing around the cheeses.
3. Drizzle honey over the Brie cheese.
4. Add clusters of grapes in between the cheeses and nuts.

5. Arrange sliced baguette around the board.

6. Garnish with fresh rosemary sprigs. Serve and enjoy!

Exotic Moroccan Cheese Board

Servings: 4-6 people | Preparation: 20 minutes

Ingredients:

- 150g (5 oz) Chevre (goat cheese)
- 150g (5 oz) Roquefort cheese
- Lavender-infused honey
- Lavender and thyme crackers
- Dried lavender buds (for visual appeal)
- Fresh lavender sprigs for garnish

Directions:

1. Place Harissa-spiced cheese and Date and almond-studded cheese on your platter.
2. Arrange Moroccan lamb meatballs and serve spicy harissa sauce in a small dish.
3. Offer warm pita bread for scooping.
4. Garnish with fresh mint leaves for a refreshing touch.

Fall Harvest Cheese Board

Servings: 4-6 people | Preparation: 20 minutes

Ingredients:

- 150g (5 oz) Aged cheddar cheese
- 150g (5 oz) Gruyère cheese
- Dried apricots
- Candied pecans
- Fresh apple slices
- Fig jam
- Multigrain crackers
- Fresh sage leaves for garnish

Directions:

1. Arrange aged cheddar and Gruyère cheeses on your serving platter.
2. Scatter dried apricots and candied pecans around the cheeses.
3. Add fresh apple slices and a dish of fig jam.
4. Serve with multigrain crackers.
5. Garnish with fresh sage leaves.

French Elegance Cheese Board

Servings: 4-6 people | Preparation: 20 minutes

Ingredients:

- 150g (5 oz) Camembert cheese
- 150g (5 oz) Roquefort cheese
- Pâté de foie gras
- Fresh baguette slices
- Fresh figs
- Dijon mustard
- Cornichons (small pickles)
- Fresh rosemary sprigs

Directions:

1. Place the Camembert and Roquefort cheeses on your platter.
2. Add slices of pâté de foie gras as an exquisite touch.
3. Arrange fresh baguette slices, fresh figs, and cornichons around the board.
4. Offer Dijon mustard as a condiment.
5. Garnish with fresh rosemary sprigs.

Greek Islands Cheese Board

Servings: 4-6 people | Preparation: 20 minutes

Ingredients:

- 150g (5 oz) Kefalotyri cheese
- 150g (5 oz) Kasseri cheese
- Loukaniko (Greek sausage)
- Greek salad ingredients (cucumbers, tomatoes, red onion, olives)
- Tzatziki sauce
- Pita bread
- Fresh dill sprigs for garnish

Directions:

1. Place Kefalotyri and Kasseri cheeses on your serving platter.
2. Slice Loukaniko (Greek sausage) into rounds and add it to the platter.
3. Create a mini Greek salad with cucumbers, tomatoes, red onion, and olives.
4. Serve tzatziki sauce with pita bread.
5. Garnish with fresh dill sprigs.

Hawaiian Luau Cheese Board

Servings: 4-6 people | Preparation: 20 minutes

Ingredients:

- 150g (5 oz) Chevre (goat cheese)

- 150g (5 oz) Roquefort cheese
- Lavender-infused honey
- Lavender and thyme crackers
- Dried lavender buds (for visual appeal)
- Fresh lavender sprigs for garnish

Directions:

1. Place Macadamia nut cheese and Coconut Gouda cheese on your serving platter.
2. Arrange fresh pineapple chunks and serve mango salsa in a small dish.
3. Sprinkle toasted coconut flakes over the cheeses.
4. Serve with sweet potato chips for an island twist.
5. Garnish with edible orchid blossoms.

Indian Spice Cheese Board

Servings: 4-6 people | Preparation: 20 minutes

Ingredients:

- 150g (5 oz) Chevre (goat cheese)
- 150g (5 oz) Roquefort cheese
- Lavender-infused honey
- Lavender and thyme crackers
- Dried lavender buds (for visual appeal)
- Fresh lavender sprigs for garnish

Directions:

1. Place cubed Paneer cheese and Garam masala-spiced cheese on your platter.
2. Offer mango chutney as a delightful accompaniment.
3. Serve with crispy papadums for scooping.
4. Accompany with fresh cucumber and mint raita.
5. Garnish with fresh coriander leaves.

Italian Delight Cheese Board

Servings: 4-6 people | Preparation: 20 minutes minutes

Ingredients:

- 150g (5 oz) Parmigiano-Reggiano cheese
- Prosciutto di Parma
- Salami
- Grilled artichoke hearts
- Marinated olives
- Sun-dried tomatoes
- Fresh basil leaves
- Breadsticks
- Balsamic glaze for drizzling

Directions:

1. Arrange the Mozzarella and Parmigiano-Reggiano cheeses on your platter.
2. Intertwine slices of Prosciutto di Parma between the cheeses.
3. Place grilled artichoke hearts, marinated olives, and sun-dried tomatoes around the board.

4. Garnish with fresh basil leaves.

5. Serve with sliced ciabatta bread and a drizzle of balsamic glaze.

Japanese Sushi and Cheese Board

Servings: 4-6 people | Preparation: 20 minutes

Ingredients:

- 150g (5 oz) Chevre (goat cheese)
- 150g (5 oz) Roquefort cheese
- Lavender-infused honey
- Lavender and thyme crackers
- Dried lavender buds (for visual appeal)
- Fresh lavender sprigs for garnish

Directions:

1. Arrange Wasabi-infused cheese and Sesame seaweed cheese on your serving platter.

2. Place sashimi-grade tuna slices between the cheeses.

3. Serve pickled ginger, soy sauce, and wasabi in small dishes.

4. Offer nori sheets for wrapping a cheese and tuna combination.

5. Garnish with fresh shiso leaves for an authentic touch.

Kid-Friendly Cheese Board

Servings: 4-6 kids | Preparation: 10 minutes

Ingredients:

- 100g (3.5 oz) Mild cheddar cheese, cut into cubes
- 100g (3.5 oz) Monterey Jack cheese, cut into cubes
- 1/2 cup (60g) baby carrots
- 1/2 cup (60g) apple slices
- 1/4 cup (60g) peanut butter
- 1/4 cup (30g) pretzels
- Celery sticks
- Grapes

Directions:

1. Arrange the cheese cubes in the center of a kid-friendly platter.

2. Surround the cheese with baby carrots and apple slices.

3. Place peanut butter in a small bowl for dipping.

4. Add pretzels and celery sticks around the platter.

5. Scatter grapes on the board.

6. Serve and watch the kids enjoy!

Luscious Cherry Blossom Cheese Board

Servings: 4-6 people | Preparation: 20 minutes

Ingredients:

- 150g (5 oz) Chevre (goat cheese)
- 150g (5 oz) Roquefort cheese
- Lavender-infused honey
- Lavender and thyme crackers
- Dried lavender buds (for visual appeal)
- Fresh lavender sprigs for garnish

Directions:

1. Place Sakura cherry blossom cheese and Yuzu citrus cheese on your platter.

2. Serve Umeboshi (pickled plums) in a small dish.
3. Arrange sake-infused pears for a delightful twist.
4. Offer miso-sesame crackers for pairing.
5. Garnish with edible cherry blossoms.

Mediterranean Mezze Cheese Board

Servings: 4-6 people | Preparation: 20 minutes

Ingredients:

- 150g (5 oz) Feta cheese
- 150g (5 oz) Halloumi cheese
- 1/2 cup of Kalamata olives
- 1/2 cup of cherry tomatoes
- 1/4 cup of hummus
- 1/4 cup of tzatziki sauce
- 1/4 cup of roasted red peppers
- Pita bread, sliced
- Fresh mint leaves for garnish

Directions:

1. Place the Feta and Halloumi cheeses on your serving platter.
2. Surround the cheeses with Kalamata olives and cherry tomatoes.
3. Spoon hummus and tzatziki sauce into small bowls and arrange them on the board.
4. Add roasted red peppers in a separate bowl.
5. Arrange slices of pita bread around the board.
6. Garnish with fresh mint leaves. Serve and enjoy!

Mediterranean Sunshine Cheese Board

Servings: 4-6 people | Preparation: 20 minutes

Ingredients:

- 150g (5 oz) Greek Feta cheese
- 150g (5 oz) Halloumi cheese
- Dolmades (stuffed grape leaves)
- Marinated artichoke hearts
- Cherry tomatoes on the vine
- Tzatziki sauce

- Warm pita bread
- Fresh oregano sprigs

Directions:

1. Arrange Greek Feta and Halloumi cheeses on your serving platter.
2. Place dolmades and marinated artichoke hearts around the cheeses.
3. Intertwine cherry tomatoes on the vine for a fresh look.
4. Serve tzatziki sauce with warm pita bread.
5. Garnish with fresh oregano sprigs.

Mexican Fiesta Cheese Board

Servings: 4-6 people | Preparation: 20 minutes minutes

Ingredients:

- 150g (5 oz) Manchego cheese
- 150g (5 oz) Cotija cheese
- Sliced chorizo
- Sliced jalapeños
- Salsa and guacamole
- Tortilla chips

Directions:

1. Place Manchego and Cotija cheeses on your serving platter.
2. Layer slices of chorizo and sliced jalapeños between the cheeses.
3. Offer small dishes of salsa and guacamole. Serve with tortilla chips.

Oceanic Seafood Cheese Board

Servings: 4-6 people | Preparation: 20 minutes

Ingredients:

- 150g (5 oz) Chevre (goat cheese)
- 150g (5 oz) Roquefort cheese
- Lavender-infused honey
- Lavender and thyme crackers
- Dried lavender buds (for visual appeal)
- Fresh lavender sprigs for garnish

Directions:

1. Arrange Smoked salmon cream cheese and Wasabi and seaweed cheese on your serving platter.
2. Place fresh oysters on the half shell between the cheeses.
3. Serve with fresh lemon wedges for squeezing over the oysters.
4. Offer water crackers for accompaniment.
5. Garnish with fresh seaweed for a taste of the sea.

Provencal Delights Cheese Board

Servings: 4-6 people | Preparation: 20 minutes

Ingredients:

- 150g (5 oz) Chevre (goat cheese)
- 150g (5 oz) Roquefort cheese
- Lavender-infused honey
- Lavender and thyme crackers
- Dried lavender buds (for visual appeal)
- Fresh lavender sprigs for garnish

Directions:

1. Arrange Chevre and Roquefort cheeses on your serving platter.
2. Drizzle lavender-infused honey over the Chevre.
3. Serve with lavender and thyme crackers.
4. Sprinkle dried lavender buds for visual appeal.
5. Garnish with fresh lavender sprigs.

Romantic Chocolate and Cheese Fondue Board

Servings: 4-6 people | Preparation: 20 minutes

Ingredients:

- 150g (5 oz) Chevre (goat cheese)
- 150g (5 oz) Roquefort cheese
- Lavender-infused honey
- Lavender and thyme crackers
- Dried lavender buds (for visual appeal)
- Fresh lavender sprigs for garnish

Directions:

1. Arrange Gouda cheese and Swiss Emmental cheese on your serving platter.
2. Melt dark chocolate for fondue in a small dish.
3. Serve with strawberries, banana slices, marshmallows, and pretzel sticks for dipping.

4. Garnish with fresh rose petals for a romantic touch.

Rustic French Wine and Cheese Board

Servings: 4-6 people | Preparation: 20 minutes

Ingredients:

- 150g (5 oz) Chevre (goat cheese)
- 150g (5 oz) Roquefort cheese
- Lavender-infused honey
- Lavender and thyme crackers
- Dried lavender buds (for visual appeal)
- Fresh lavender sprigs for garnish

Directions:

1. Place Saint-André triple cream cheese and Roquefort cheese on your platter.
2. Layer slices of smoked duck breast between the cheeses.
3. Serve fig and walnut preserves in a small dish.
4. Offer crusty baguette slices for a rustic touch.
5. Garnish with fresh thyme sprigs.

Scandinavian Smorgasbord Cheese Board

Servings: 4-6 people | Preparation: 20 minutes

Ingredients:

- 150g (5 oz) Norwegian Jarlsberg cheese
- 150g (5 oz) Danish Havarti cheese
- Smoked salmon
- Pickled herring
- Lingonberry jam
- Rye crispbread
- Fresh dill sprigs for garnish

Directions:

1. Place Norwegian Jarlsberg and Danish Havarti cheeses on your serving platter.
2. Roll up slices of smoked salmon and arrange them around the cheeses.
3. Offer pickled herring and lingonberry jam in small dishes.
4. Serve with rye crispbread.
5. Garnish with fresh dill sprigs.

Spanish Tapas Cheese Board

Servings: 4-6 people | Preparation: 20 minutes

Ingredients:

- 150g (5 oz) Manchego cheese
- 150g (5 oz) Mahón cheese
- Serrano ham
- Stuffed olives
- Marcona almonds
- Tomato-rubbed toast (pan con tomate)
- Fresh parsley sprigs for garnish

Directions:

1. Arrange Manchego and Mahón cheeses on your platter.
2. Drape slices of Serrano ham over the cheeses.
3. Scatter stuffed olives and Marcona almonds around the board.
4. Serve tomato-rubbed toast as a classic accompaniment.
5. Garnish with fresh parsley sprigs.

Spice and Smoke Cheese Board

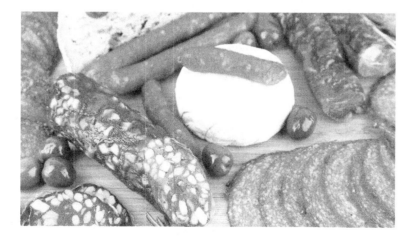

Servings: 4-6 people | Preparation: 15 minutes

Ingredients:

- 150g (5 oz) Smoked Gouda cheese
- 150g (5 oz) Pepper Jack cheese

- Soppressata or chorizo
- Spicy pickles
- Jalapeño peppers
- Mango chutney
- Crackers with seeds
- Fresh cilantro leaves

Directions:

1. Place Smoked Gouda and Pepper Jack cheeses on your serving platter.
2. Layer slices of soppressata or chorizo between the cheeses.
3. Scatter spicy pickles, jalapeño peppers, and mango chutney around the board.
4. Add crackers with seeds to complement the flavors.
5. Garnish with fresh cilantro leaves.

Sweet and Savory Cheese Board

Servings: 4-6 people | Preparation: 20 minutes

Ingredients:

- 150g (5 oz) Gorgonzola cheese
- 150g (5 oz) Manchego cheese
- 1/2 cup (120ml) of fig preserves
- 1/2 cup (120g) of dried apricots
- 1/4 cup (60ml) of honey
- 1/4 cup (30g) of candied pecans
- Whole grain crackers
- Fresh thyme sprigs for garnish

Directions:

1. Arrange the Gorgonzola and Manchego cheeses on your serving platter.
2. Surround the cheeses with fig preserves and dried apricots.
3. Drizzle honey over the Gorgonzola.
4. Add candied pecans in between the cheeses and fruits.
5. Place whole grain crackers around the board.
6. Garnish with fresh thyme sprigs.
7. Serve and savor the sweet and savory combination!

Tex-Mex Cheese Board

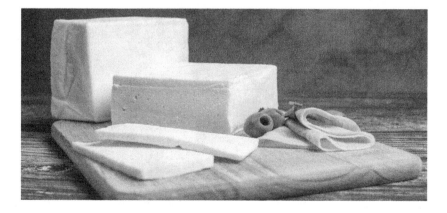

Servings: 4-6 people | Preparation: 20 minutes

Ingredients:

- 150g (5 oz) Queso fresco
- 150g (5 oz) Pepper Jack cheese
- Chorizo sausage
- Corn chips
- Sliced jalapeños
- Fresh avocado and lime wedges
- Fresh cilantro leaves for garnish

Directions:

1. Place Queso fresco and Pepper Jack cheeses on your platter.
2. Slice chorizo sausage into rounds and add it to the platter.
3. Serve with corn chips for dipping.
4. Scatter sliced jalapeños around the board.
5. Serve with fresh avocado and lime wedges.
6. Garnish with fresh cilantro leaves.

The Gourmet Cheese Board

Servings: 4-6 people | Preparation: 20 minutes minutes

Ingredients:

- 150g (5 oz) Triple cream brie
- 150g (5 oz) Stilton cheese
- Prosciutto di Parma
- Fresh black figs
- Truffle honey
- Almond and rosemary crackers
- Fresh thyme sprigs for garnish

Directions:

1. Arrange triple cream brie and Stilton cheeses on your serving platter.
2. Layer slices of Prosciutto di Parma between the cheeses.
3. Scatter fresh black figs on the board.
4. Drizzle truffle honey over the brie.
5. Serve with almond and rosemary crackers.
6. Garnish with fresh thyme sprigs.

The Spicy Southwestern Cheese Board

Servings: 4-6 people | Preparation: 20 minutes

Ingredients:

- 150g (5 oz) Chevre (goat cheese)
- 150g (5 oz) Roquefort cheese
- Lavender-infused honey
- Lavender and thyme crackers
- Dried lavender buds (for visual appeal)
- Fresh lavender sprigs for garnish

Directions:

1. Place Harissa-spiced cheese and Date and almond-studded cheese on your platter.
2. Arrange Moroccan lamb meatballs and serve spicy harissa sauce in a small dish.
3. Offer warm pita bread for scooping.
4. Garnish with fresh mint leaves for a refreshing touch.

Vegan Delight Cheese Board

Servings: 4-6 people | Preparation: 15 minutes

Ingredients:

- 150g (5 oz) Vegan cashew-based cheese
- 150g (5 oz) Vegan almond-based cheese
- 1/2 cup of mixed berries
- 1/2 cup of assorted raw veggies (carrots, cucumber, cherry tomatoes)
- 1/4 cup of hummus (vegan)
- 1/4 cup of almond butter
- Sliced baguette or gluten-free crackers
- Fresh basil leaves for garnish

Directions:

1. Place the vegan cheeses on your serving platter.
2. Arrange mixed berries in between the cheeses.
3. Surround the cheeses with assorted raw veggies.
4. Spoon vegan hummus and almond butter into small bowls and place them on the board. Arrange slices of baguette or gluten-free crackers around the board.
5. Garnish with fresh basil leaves.
6. Serve and enjoy!

Vegan Mediterranean Cheese Board

Servings: 4-6 people | Preparation: 20 minutes

Ingredients:

- 150g (5 oz) Vegan almond-based feta
- 150g (5 oz) Vegan tofu-based halloumi
- Stuffed vine leaves
- Kalamata olives
- Cucumber and bell pepper sticks
- Vegan tzatziki sauce

- Gluten-free crackers
- Fresh dill for garnish

Directions:

1. Place vegan almond-based feta and tofu-based halloumi on your platter.
2. Arrange stuffed vine leaves and Kalamata olives around the vegan cheeses.
3. Add cucumber and bell pepper sticks for freshness.
4. Serve vegan tzatziki sauce with gluten-free crackers.
5. Garnish with fresh dill sprigs.

Chapter 10:
Cheese Cutting Guide and More

Expert Tips on Cutting Cheese: Slice with Precision

One of the most critical aspects of creating an exceptional cheese board is the art of cutting cheese. Properly slicing and presenting cheese enhances the overall aesthetic and taste of your board. In this section, we'll explore expert tips on how to slice cheese with precision and finesse.

1. Choose the Right Tools

Before chopping cheese, you need the correct instruments. Cheese knives must be sharp and high-quality. Cheese knives vary in effectiveness. Cheese planes work well for semi-hard cheeses like Gouda and Swiss, while wire cheese slicers work well for softer cheeses like Brie and Camembert.

2. Serve Cheese at the Right Temperature

How easy cheese is to cut depends on its temperature. For optimum results, serve cheese at the right temperature. Usually 30 minutes before serving, remove it from the fridge. Extremely cold cheese may crumble, while extremely warm cheese is too soft and messy to slice.

3. Cut Cheese at an Angle

Angle the knife blade to slice cheese thinly and evenly. This method increases cheese surface area, letting your taste senses interact more. Avoid disintegrating old cheddar and Parmesan by slicing at a little slant.

4. Adapt Your Technique for Different Cheese Types

Each type of cheese has its unique characteristics, and therefore, you may need to adjust your cutting technique accordingly:

- **Soft Cheeses:** Soft, creamy cheeses like Brie should be cut with a wire cheese slicer or a knife with a thin blade. Start from the outer edge and work your way to the center, creating wedges.
- **Semi-Hard Cheeses:** Semi-hard cheeses like Gouda or Monterey Jack are best cut into thin slices using a cheese plane or a sharp knife. Cut perpendicular to the rind to create even pieces.
- **Hard Cheeses:** Aged cheeses like Parmesan require a more robust knife. You can use a cheese cleaver to break off pieces or a sharp chef's knife to create thin shards.
- **Blue-Veined Cheeses:** For crumbly blue cheeses like Roquefort or Gorgonzola, a cheese wire is your best friend. Gently cut through the cheese to avoid excessive crumbling.
5. Keep Your Knife Clean

To maintain the integrity of your cheese board, ensure that you clean your knife between different cheese varieties. Cross-contamination can negatively impact the flavors of your cheeses, so always wipe your knife with a damp cloth or rinse it between cuts.

Guides on Pairing Cheese and Condiments: Creating Flavor Synergy

Pairing cheese with complementary condiments can elevate the taste and experience of your cheese board. Here, we'll provide you with guidance on creating flavor synergy between cheeses and a variety of accompaniments.

1. The Power of Contrast

When it comes to pairing cheeses and condiments, contrast can be a potent tool. Consider the following combinations:

- **Sweet and Savory:** The sweetness of fruit preserves or honey can beautifully contrast the saltiness of aged cheeses like Gouda or Parmesan.
- **Creamy and Crunchy:** Pair creamy, soft cheeses with crispy accompaniments like crackers or crostini. The contrast in texture enhances the overall enjoyment.
- **Acidic and Creamy:** Acidic condiments such as pickles or mustard can cut through the richness of creamy cheeses like Camembert or triple cream Brie.
2. Consider Regional Pairings

Matching cheese and condiments based on their regional origins can create harmonious flavor profiles. For example:

- **Italian Cheese with Balsamic Vinegar:** Pair Parmesan or Pecorino with a drizzle of aged balsamic vinegar for an Italian-inspired combination.
- **French Cheese with Fig Jam:** French cheeses like Brie or Roquefort pair wonderfully with fig jam, a classic French accompaniment.
- **Spanish Cheese with Quince Paste:** Manchego cheese and quince paste are a beloved combination in Spanish cuisine.
3. Experiment with Texture and Flavor

Try different textures and tastes. Mix sweet, savory, and spicy condiments to satisfy varied tastes. Almonds and walnuts offer crunch, while olives and capers give brininess to your cheese board.

4. Include Fresh and Dried Fruits

Fresh and dried fruits are fantastic companions for cheese. Fresh grapes, apple slices, or pear wedges can provide a refreshing contrast to the richness of cheese. Dried fruits like apricots, figs, or dates add a concentrated burst of sweetness.

5. Serve with Bread and Crackers

Bread and crackers are staples on cheese boards. Opt for a variety of options, including baguette slices, whole-grain crackers, and gluten-free choices to accommodate different dietary preferences.

6. Presentation Matters

When serving cheese and condiments, presentation matters. Arrange the condiments in small dishes or ramekins to keep them separate and prevent the flavors from melding. Labeling each condiment can also be a thoughtful touch for your guests.

Notes on Aging, Seasoning, and Presentation: Craftsmanship Matters

As you delve deeper into the world of cheese boards, it's essential to appreciate the craftsmanship of cheese. Understanding the aging process, seasoning, and the art of presentation can help you create a memorable cheese board experience.

1. Aging and Its Influence

Aging affects cheese taste and texture. Age impacts cheese's flavor, consistency, and scent. Consider these factors while choosing board cheeses:

- **Fresh Cheeses:** These are young, soft cheeses with a mild flavor and a high moisture content. They include varieties like ricotta, mozzarella, and goat cheese.
- **Semi-Hard Cheeses:** Semi-hard cheeses like cheddar and Gouda have undergone

moderate aging, resulting in a firmer texture and more pronounced flavors.

- **Hard Cheeses:** Aged cheeses like Parmesan or Pecorino are firm, dry, and packed with intense, concentrated flavors.
- **Blue-Veined Cheeses:** These cheeses, such as Roquefort or Stilton, develop their characteristic blue veins through the introduction of specific molds during aging.

2. Seasoning Your Cheese Board

Seasoning your cheese board is an opportunity to enhance the flavors and presentation. Consider sprinkling fresh herbs, such as rosemary or thyme, over your cheese for a touch of freshness. Drizzles of high-quality olive oil or a dusting of black pepper can also elevate the taste.

3. Craft an Artful Presentation

The visual aspect of your cheese board is just as important as its taste. A well-arranged board is a feast for the eyes. Here are some presentation tips:

- **Symmetry and Balance:** Arrange the cheeses and accompaniments in a balanced manner, creating a visually pleasing composition.
- **Color Variety:** Incorporate colorful fruits, vegetables, and condiments to add vibrancy to your board.
- **Layer and Stack:** Experiment with stacking or layering ingredients to create depth and dimension on your board.
- **Wooden Boards and Platters:** Wooden boards or platters make an excellent canvas for your cheese board, adding rustic charm.
- **Edible Garnishes:** Edible garnishes, such as edible flowers or microgreens, can add a final touch of elegance.

Appreciating cheese's artistry, seasoning it, and presenting it well can turn your cheese board into a sensory experience.

These professional techniques will help you make tasty, attractive, and flavorful cheese boards. Mastering cheese cutting and paring will improve your cheese board game, regardless of your expertise.

BONUS:
Low Risk, High Reward

Budget-Friendly Cheese Board Solutions: Flavor Without Breaking the Bank

Creating cheese boards that are both flavorful and budget-friendly is not only possible but also a delightful challenge for any culinary enthusiast. In this chapter, we'll explore a variety of tips and tricks to craft impressive cheese compositions without straining your wallet. Let's embark on a journey to discover how to make the most of your resources while treating your taste buds to a symphony of flavors.

1. **Strategic Cheese Selection:** Begin by choosing cheeses that offer value without compromising taste. Opt for versatile and cost-effective options like cheddar, mozzarella, or Swiss. These cheeses provide a fantastic base for your board while staying budget-conscious.

2. **DIY Accompaniments:** Embrace the art of making your own accompaniments. Whip up homemade spreads, sauces, or jams using simple ingredients from your pantry. It's not only cost-effective but also a wonderful way to personalize your

cheese board.

3. **Seasonal and Local Produce:** Leverage the seasonality of fruits and vegetables in your region. Fresh, local produce tends to be more affordable and offers a vibrant, seasonal twist to your board. Think apples in the fall, berries in the summer, or asparagus in the spring.

4. **Store Brands and Sales:** Don't overlook store brands or discounted items when shopping for your cheese board. These can often be of high quality while being budget-friendly. Keep an eye out for sales and special offers to further reduce costs.

5. **Creative Repurposing:** Reimagine leftovers and food scraps as ingredients for your cheese board. Stale bread can become croutons, and leftover herbs can be infused into homemade spreads. Reducing food waste while enhancing your board is a win-win.

6. **Thrift Shop Finds:** Visit thrift stores or second-hand shops for unique and budget-friendly serving platters, cheese knives, and decorations. You'll be surprised at the charming pieces you can discover to elevate your presentation.

7. **Minimalism with Impact:** Sometimes, less is more. Focus on a smaller selection of high-quality, budget-friendly items rather than overloading your board with expensive options. A few well-chosen cheeses and accompaniments can still create a delightful experience.

Creating budget-friendly cheese boards is about ingenuity and thoughtful planning. With these strategies in your culinary toolkit, you can enjoy the art of cheese compositions without worrying about your wallet. So, embark on your cheese board adventure, and savor the flavors of frugality.

Recipes for Complementary Condiments

Balsamic Fig Jam

Servings: 8 | Preparation: 10 minutes | Cooking: 15 minutes

Ingredients:

- 10 fresh figs, diced
- 1/2 cup (120ml) balsamic vinegar
- 1/2 cup (100g) brown sugar
- 1/4 cup (60ml) water
- 1 teaspoon lemon zest
- 1/2 teaspoon cinnamon

Directions:

1. In a saucepan, the figs, balsamic vinegar, brown sugar, water, lemon zest, and cinnamon are combined.
2. Simmer the mixture over a low heat, intermittently stirring, for around 15 minutes until it reaches a thick consistency.

3. Remove the mixture from the heat source and let it to cool down.
4. Serve the dish with cheese and crackers.

Caramelized Onion and Rosemary Butter

Servings: 8 | Preparation: 15 minutes | Cooking: 30 minutes

Ingredients:

- 2 large onions, thinly sliced
- 4 tablespoons (60g) butter
- 2 sprigs fresh rosemary
- Salt and pepper to taste

Directions:

1. Melt the butter in a large pan over medium-low heat.
2. Add the thinly sliced onions and simmer for approximately 30 minutes, stirring now and again, until they are soft and caramelized.
3. Cook for a further five minutes after adding salt, pepper, and fresh rosemary leaves.

4. Allow the liquid to cool before blending it smoothly with a hand blender.

5. Use as a spread on crackers or toast.

Cilantro-Lime Hummus

Servings: 8 | Preparation: 10 minutes | Cooking: 5 minutes

Ingredients:

- 1 cup (240g) classic hummus
- Zest and juice of 1 lime
- 1/4 cup (60ml) fresh coriander, finely chopped
- 1/2 teaspoon (2.5g) ground cumin
- Salt and pepper to taste

Directions:

1. Start by grabbing a bowl. Throw in some classic hummus, lime zest, lime juice, fresh cilantro, ground cumin, a pinch of salt, and a dash of pepper.

2. Mix everything together until it's all nicely blended.

3. Time to enjoy! Use it as a dip with pita, veggies, or as a side for your cheese platter.

Classic Caesar Dressing

Servings: 8 | Preparation: 10 minutes | Cooking: 5 minutes

Ingredients:

- 1/2 cup (120ml) mayonnaise
- 2 tablespoons (30g) grated Parmesan cheese
- 1 tablespoon (15ml) Dijon mustard
- 1 clove garlic, minced
- 2 tablespoons (30ml) fresh lemon juice
- 1/2 teaspoon Worcestershire sauce
- Salt and pepper to taste

Directions:

1. To begin, take a bowl and combine the following ingredients: mayonnaise, grated Parmesan cheese, Dijon mustard, chopped garlic, freshly squeezed lemon juice, Worcestershire sauce, salt, and pepper.
2. Taste it, and then modify the taste and the consistency to your satisfaction.

3. You may use this dressing to make traditional Caesar salads or as a drizzle for your cheese board. Both work really well. Have fun!

Cucumber and Dill Yogurt Dip

Servings: 8 | Preparation: 10 minutes | Cooking: 15 minutes

Ingredients:

- 1 cup (240g) Greek yogurt
- 1 cucumber, finely diced
- 2 tablespoons (30ml) fresh dill, finely chopped
- 1 clove garlic, minced
- 1 teaspoon (5ml) lemon juice
- Salt and pepper to taste

Directions:

1. Get a bowl, toss in some Greek yogurt, finely dice some cucumber, chop up fresh dill, mince some garlic, squeeze in lemon juice, and sprinkle a bit of salt and pepper.

2. Stir everything up until it's all nicely mixed together.

3. Now, you've got yourself a cool yogurt dip, perfect for dunking your veggies or pairing with your cheese platter. Enjoy!

Honey-Dijon Mustard

Servings: 8 | Preparation: 5 minutes | Cooking: 5 minutes

Ingredients:

- 1/4 cup (60ml) Dijon mustard
- 2 tablespoons (30ml) honey
- 1 tablespoon (15ml) white wine vinegar
- 1/2 teaspoon (2.5g) garlic powder
- Salt and pepper to taste

Directions:

1. Start by whisking Dijon mustard, honey, white wine vinegar, garlic powder, salt, and pepper in a little bowl.

2. Taste it, and if you want it sweeter or tangier, adjust it to your liking.

3. Use it as a dip or drizzle it over your cheese board. Enjoy!

Lemon-Herb Infused Olive Oil

Servings: 8 | Preparation: 10 minutes | Cooking: 5 minutes

Ingredients:

- 1 cup (240ml) extra-virgin olive oil
- Zest of 1 lemon
- 2 cloves garlic, minced
- 2 sprigs fresh rosemary, thyme, or your choice of herbs
- Salt and pepper to taste

Directions:

1. Start by warming up some olive oil in a little saucepan over low heat.
2. Toss in lemon zest, minced garlic, and fresh herbs.
3. Let it gently simmer for about 5 minutes, then take it off the heat and let it cool down.
4. After it's cooled, strain the oil to get rid of the herbs and garlic.
5. Now, you've got a tasty oil to serve in a small dish for dipping bread or drizzling over cheese. Enjoy!

Lemon-Poppy Seed Dressing

Servings: 8 | Preparation: 10 minutes | Cooking: 5 minutes

Ingredients:

- 1/4 cup (60ml) fresh lemon juice
- 1/4 cup (60ml) olive oil
- 2 tablespoons (30ml) honey
- 1 tablespoon (15g) poppy seeds
- 1 teaspoon Dijon mustard
- Salt and pepper to taste

Directions:

1. In a small bowl, whisk together fresh lemon juice, olive oil, honey, poppy seeds, Dijon mustard, salt, and pepper.

2. Adjust the sweetness and tanginess to your liking.

3. Serve as a dressing for salads or drizzle over cheese.

Raspberry Balsamic Reduction

Servings: 8 | Preparation: 5 minutes | Cooking: 15 minutes

Ingredients:

- 1 cup (150g) fresh raspberries
- 1/2 cup (120ml) balsamic vinegar
- 2 tablespoons (30ml) honey

Directions:

1. Take a saucepan.
2. Put raspberries, balsamic vinegar, and honey in it.
3. Heat it up over medium heat.
4. Let it simmer for around 15 minutes, stirring every now and then, until it thickens up.

5. Once it's done, take it off the heat.

6. Strain out those pesky raspberry seeds.

7. Allow it to cool down.

8. When it's cool, you can serve it up with some cheese. Enjoy!

Red Pepper and Walnut Dip

Servings: 8 | Preparation: 10 minutes | Cooking: 5 minutes

Ingredients:

- 1 cup (240ml) roasted red peppers (from a jar), drained and chopped
- 1/2 cup (60g) toasted walnuts
- 2 cloves garlic
- 2 tablespoons (30ml) olive oil
- 1 tablespoon (15ml) lemon juice
- 1 teaspoon paprika
- Salt and pepper to taste

Directions:

1. Start by tossing roasted red peppers, toasted walnuts, garlic, olive oil, lemon juice, paprika, salt, and pepper into a food processor.
2. Give it a good blend until you reach the texture you like.
3. Now, you're all set to use it as a dip for your veggies or crackers. Enjoy!

Roasted Garlic and Tomato Chutney

Servings: 8 | Preparation: 10 minutes | Cooking: 30 minutes

Ingredients:

- 2 bulbs of garlic
- 240ml (1 cup) cherry tomatoes
- 30ml (2 tablespoons) olive oil
- 15ml (1 tablespoon) balsamic vinegar
- 5g (1 teaspoon) brown sugar
- Salt and pepper to taste

Directions:

1. Preheat your oven to 375°F (190°C).
2. Slice off the top of each garlic head to expose the cloves, drizzle with olive oil, and wrap in aluminum foil.
3. Toss cherry tomatoes with olive oil, balsamic vinegar, brown sugar, salt, and pepper. Place the wrapped garlic heads and the tomatoes on a baking sheet.
4. Roast for about 30 minutes or until the garlic is soft and the tomatoes are blistered.
5. Let them cool, then squeeze the roasted garlic cloves out of the skins.
6. Mash the garlic cloves with the roasted tomatoes.
7. Serve as a savory chutney with your cheese board.

Spicy Mango Chutney

Servings: 8 | Preparation: 15 minutes | Cooking: 20 minutes

Ingredients:

- 2 ripe mangoes, peeled, pitted, and diced
- 1/2 cup (100g) caster sugar
- 1/4 cup (60ml) apple cider vinegar
- 1/4 cup (60ml) water
- 1 teaspoon (5g) fresh ginger, minced

- 1/4 teaspoon (1.25g) red pepper flakes

Directions:

1. Start by grabbing a saucepan. Toss in some mangoes, sugar, apple cider vinegar, water, minced ginger, and a pinch of red pepper flakes.
2. Fire it up and get the mix boiling. Then, turn down the heat and let it simmer for about 20 minutes. Stir from time to time until it thickens up.
3. Give it some time to cool down, and when it's ready, pop it into an airtight container.
4. Now, you're all set to serve it up with some cheese and your favorite crackers. Enjoy!

Strawberry and Mint Salsa

Servings: 8 | Preparation: 10 minutes | Cooking: 5 minutes

Ingredients:

- 1 cup (240ml) fresh strawberries, diced
- 2 tablespoons (30ml) fresh mint, finely chopped
- 1 tablespoon (15ml) red onion, finely minced
- 1 teaspoon (5ml) honey
- Zest and juice of 1 lime
- Salt and pepper to taste

Directions:

1. Start by taking a bowl and throwing in some diced strawberries, fresh mint, minced red onion, honey, lime zest, lime juice, a pinch of salt, and a dash of pepper.
2. Give it all a gentle mix to make sure everything gets friendly with each other.
3. Now, you're all set to serve up this delightful fruit salsa alongside your cheese board. Enjoy!

Sun-Dried Tomato Pesto

Servings: 8 | Preparation: 10 minutes | Cooking: 5 minutes

Ingredients:

- 1 cup (240ml) sun-dried tomatoes (in oil), drained
- 1/4 cup (15g) fresh basil leaves
- 2 cloves garlic
- 1/4 cup (25g) grated Parmesan cheese
- 1/4 cup (30g) pine nuts, toasted
- 1/4 cup (60ml) olive oil
- Salt and pepper to taste

Directions:

1. Pop your sun-dried tomatoes, fresh basil leaves, garlic, grated Parmesan cheese, toasted pine nuts, olive oil, salt, and pepper into a food processor.
2. Give it a whirl in the processor until it's just the way you like it.
3. Now, you've got yourself a tasty pesto to serve with your cheese board. Enjoy!

Sweet and Spicy Pineapple Salsa

Servings: 8 | Preparation: 10 minutes | Cooking: 5 minutes

Ingredients:

- 1 cup (240ml) fresh pineapple, diced
- 1/4 cup (60ml) red bell pepper, finely chopped
- 1/4 cup (60ml) red onion, finely minced
- 1 jalapeño pepper, seeded and minced
- 2 tablespoons (30ml) fresh cilantro, finely chopped
- 1 tablespoon (15ml) lime juice
- 1 teaspoon (5ml) honey
- Salt and pepper to taste

Directions:

1. To prepare, mix sliced pineapple, red bell pepper, chopped onion, minced jalapeño pepper, cilantro, lime juice, honey, salt, and pepper on a plate.
2. Make care to combine well to create a balanced sweet-spicy flavor.
3. Tangy salsa may now be displayed near the cheese board. Enjoy it!

Conclusion

As we conclude our cheese board excursion, we may reflect on the delicious experience. The Cheese Board Cookbook unleashes creativity, taste, and delight in cooking. You and your family will enjoy your new cheese-making skills for years to come.

Embracing the Versatility and Creativity of Cheese Compositions

Cheese boards are versatile. The possibilities are endless whether it comes to dazzling guests at a formal party, treating your family to a night in, or constructing a healthy and delectable board for your kids. Mix tastes, textures, and colors to be creative.

You've also mastered pairing cheeses with several foods. From tempting sauces and spreads to sweet and savory jams, croutons, mustards, and pickles, your cheese boards may now wow the table.

Happy Cheesemongering!

After reading this book and learning from its experiences, start your own cheese board adventures. On a nice night in, a noisy party, or a peaceful evening with friends and family, your cheese creations will be the spotlight.

Cheese boards are more than yummy. Creativeness, presentation, and sharing these tasty combinations are crucial. Consider every cheese blend a gastronomic masterpiece. Enjoy cheese boards' endless possibilities as you begin your new culinary journey. Taste various cheeses, pairings, and flavors to surprise your taste buds.

Please pick your favorite cheeses, choose your accompaniments, and serve them creatively. Celebrate your masterpieces with loved ones and watch their faces light up. Cheese compositions are limitless—create, explore, and enjoy. With additional knowledge, cheese board alternatives are unlimited. Good cheesemongering, and may your cheese boards provide joy, flavor, and togetherness for years.

References:

Images: Freepik.com.

Some images within this book were chosen using resources from Freepik.com

Made in the USA
Las Vegas, NV
16 November 2023

80935980R00057